Suc[illegible]arents

School of the Word

Titles in the School of the Word series:

A Life of Worship	John Johnson & Mike Stevens
According to Your Faith	Bryn Jones
Battle for the Mind	Stephen Matthew
Be Eager to Prophesy	Hugh Thompson
Called to be a Disciple	Dale Barnes
Christian Manhood	David Matthew
Effective Prayer	Bryn Jones
Essential Foundations	Hugh Thompson
Excelling as a Woman	Barbie Reynolds
Fulfilment in Marriage	Hugh & Rosemary Thompson
Go and Make Disciples	Hugh Thompson
Issues Facing Society	John Houghton
Living in the Anointing	Paul Scanlon
Money Matters	Stephen Matthew
More Than Conquerors	Don Silber
Realities of the New Creation	Dale Barnes
Secure in God	Tony & Margaret Howson
Successful Parents	Hugh & Rosemary Thompson
Woman: Created for Success	Barbie Reynolds
Woman: Living in Victory	Barbie Reynolds

Successful Parents

Hugh & Rosemary Thompson

Harvestime

Published in the United Kingdom by:
Harvestime Publishing Ltd, 69 Main Street
Markfield, Leicester LE6 0UT

First published by Harvestime under the title
Successful Parenthood
First printed April 1989
Reprinted January 1992

ISBN 1-872877-07-9

Typeset in the United Kingdom by:
ScribeTech Ltd, Bradford BD8 7BX

Printed and bound in Great Britain by:
BPCC Hazell Books, Aylesbury
Bucks, England
Member of BPCC Ltd

Increasing numbers of people are wanting to study the Word of God in depth. To go to a Bible college or seminary is not feasible for the majority, yet they desire more than the average church is able to provide in its teaching curriculum.

The book you are about to study is part of a library of components that together provide a comprehensive overview of the Scriptures in relation to life. Each book is complete in itself but is developed in such a way that the best result is experienced by studying it as part of the whole series.

We have produced the curriculum so that each component, in addition to its use as a personal study, can provide a seven-week teaching programme for study in church, home, college campus, school, military base, prison or any other group setting.

It is our prayer that you will be greatly enriched in your spiritual development through this book.

Bryn Jones
Founder — School of the Word

Getting the Most Out of This Study

This School of the Word study book is one of a series designed to relate Bible truths to everyday life. Each of the seven lessons starts with a direct search of the Scriptures and ends with a challenge to the student to apply the truths discovered. As the blank spaces left in Bible verses are filled in, the most important words and phrases stand out clearly on the page.

The material can be used in a number of different ways. It can form the basis of an individual study or be used in a group setting over a number of weeks. But experience has shown that it has the greatest benefit when a group of people study it together under a leader who is well prepared.

Tips for Leaders

If you are a leader planning to take a number of people through this study, you should consider the following:

1. Be prepared

It is essential that you do the whole study in advance yourself. This will help you to be conversant with the basic outline and have a feeling for the level of teaching based on it that your students can take.

2. Keep to the outline

It is important to keep to the outline contained in this study. This has been carefully designed to build principle on principle, 'precept upon precept' (Isaiah 28:10 RAV), with the eventual aim of the student becoming 'thoroughly equipped for every good work' (2 Timothy 3:17).

Whatever happens, don't allow your teaching to digress and become an opportunity to preach an hour's sermon!

3. Use your own experience

Even though you are staying with the outline, where possible introduce additional illustrations and applications drawn from your own experience. This makes the basic teaching more relevant to the local setting. In addition, you may wish to add more emphasis to certain points.

4. Avoid indigestion

Each lesson should take about an hour to complete. You may like to divide this into two half-hour sessions by arranging a short break for coffee and a chat halfway through. That way, the teaching is kept to manageable portions.

In some cases you may feel that the group discussion is of such vital importance to your local area that you want to spread each lesson over two weeks. If you do this, try to divide the questions at the end so that they are relevant to that week's teaching.

5. Have the right tools

Make sure that all the students have access to a copy of the New International Version of the Bible — upon which the book is based. Encourage them to fill in the blank spaces in advance but to leave answering the true/false questions until after each teaching session.

Tips for Students

Before you start the study you need to ask yourself: Am I really committed to growing as a disciple of Jesus Christ? If the answer is yes, then you're ready to proceed. Here are some immediate steps you can take to ensure maximum benefit from the course:

1. Determine your goal

This book is designed to help you achieve God's goal and destiny for you. It doesn't matter whether you are young or old, a recent convert or someone who has been a Christian for many years.

Today you are taking a step towards the fulfilment of your destiny.

Look ahead and see yourself as God desires you to be. Then confess your commitment: 'This is the kind of person I *will* become.'

2. Plan your progress

Your faith commitment to work through this book, and so take one more step towards becoming the person God intends you to be, must not only be pursued but measured in its progress. The apostle Paul said:

> *'By the grace given me I say to every one of you: Do not think of yourself more highly than you ought, but rather think of yourself with sober judgment, in accordance with the measure of faith God has given you.'*
>
> (Romans 12:3)

You know the kind of person you already are. You know the level of commitment you already have in your life. Now from this point determine how much time per day or week you are prepared to give to the study of the Word of God to achieve your goal.

At the end of each lesson in this study-book there is an opportunity for you to complete assignments and answer some Bible-based questions. This helps to fix the Word of God more firmly in your heart, and thus provide a reservoir of truth that the Holy Spirit can draw upon in the training of your life.

3. Recruit to the study course

Fellowship is one of the keys to Christian growth. The word 'fellowship' comes from the Greek word *koinonia*, which means to 'share things in common'.

Nothing will facilitate your progress as much as encouraging others to share in the same study programme with you, either on a personal basis or in a group. Share with each other the things you are learning and discovering in the Word of God and in life.

In this way you will be able to practise together much of what you study, and so strengthen each other in faith, just as 'iron sharpens iron' (Proverbs 27:17).

4. Set and maintain your standards

If this study is to be of maximum benefit to you, it must not be hurried. It is no use merely reading the written material and rushing the assignment. The book is designed to provoke you to your own searching and thinking, and to a demonstration of faith in God.

5. Check your progress

Once you have worked right through the book, ask your pastor or church leader to read through your answers. If he is satisfied that you have done your best to complete the questions, get him to send us a note to this effect. We will then forward a certificate for him to sign and present to you.

Your pastor is also the best person to monitor your progress and share your zeal to develop as a Christian disciple. If you are at college, university or in the armed forces, or for some other reason have no immediate access to a pastor, send us your book enclosing return postage and we will send it back to you with your certificate.

School of the Word
Harvestime Publishing Ltd
69 Main Street
Markfield
Leicester LE6 0UT
UK

Contents

Unless otherwise stated, Scripture quotations are taken from the New International Version.

Other versions referred to in this series include the New American Standard Bible (NASB), the Revised Authorised Version (RAV) and the Amplified Bible (Amp).

Verses have blank spaces for you to insert the missing words as you follow the Scriptures. This will deepen the impact of the Bible in your life.

A Rewarding Responsibility

Why do people become parents? For all sorts of reasons. Lots of babies are conceived unplanned. Some couples beget offspring because it's their expected duty, perhaps to supply grandchildren 'while our parents can appreciate them'. We also know several mothers who opted for a full set of living dolls behind whom they could hide away from personal growth and social responsibilities!

But, of course, many parents pray and plan to train up sons and daughters as men and women of God who will contribute effectively to his purposes for their generation.

Whatever our reason for having a family, now that we have one, all of us parents have the same responsibility in our calling. We will consider that responsibility in detail in these seven lessons.

It will help if we start at the end: what do we aim to achieve through our parenting?

1. Scriptural Indications

Child psychiatrists and paediatricians have supplied the secular market with books abounding in helpful advice on how to bring up children. Some of their ideas contradict the Scriptures, but much of their counsel is sound because it is based on a lifetime's close observation of thousands of parents and children. In fact, there isn't a particle of vital truth that they have written which was not already set forth in God's Word.

But we shall have to go to the Bible to discover the nature and purpose of our calling as *Christian* parents.

a. Our job — a divine stewardship

God's purpose for us as parents is most aptly expressed in what Pharaoh's daughter said to Moses' mother on the banks of the Nile:

> *'Take this baby and nurse him for me, and I will pay you.'*
>
> (Exodus 2:9)

In fact, that entire incident describes our situation as Christian parents. The king's daughter, having saved a doomed infant, offers him back to his natural mother to nurture him as a short-term stewardship. And that is exactly the essence of Christian parenthood. The Son of God came from the royal residence of heaven to rescue our children from the edict against Adam's race. Now he offers them back into our welcoming arms under contract, on loan, for they actually belong to him.

These are his terms of contract: Take this child away from the world's rat race and nurture him *for me*, and I will give you as wages untold blessings for all the efforts of love you invest in him (or her) during the few brief years that he is your responsibility. Bring him up *for me*. No secular book on child guidance mentions *that* as the starting point. Yet this simple key transforms how we treat our children.

'I'm going home from this family-life seminar,' announced one mother, 'to speak to my children from now on as I would address my neighbour's children — with much more respect and no nagging.' Wouldn't we all show more respect if we reminded ourselves that they are the *King's* kids?

b. Our resources — the Spirit and the Word

It all sounds too much, a daunting and formidable task. We feel alarmed, like the virgin Mary when she first faced the commission to bring up the Son of the Most High: 'How will this be?' (Luke 1:34). The answer given to her is sufficient promise to us also: '*The Holy Spirit* will come upon you' (v35); to which she responded: 'May it be to me as *you have said*' (v38).

The Spirit of God and the Word of God will equip us with wisdom and ability for the job in hand. Paul's advice to parents in Ephesus,

> *'Be __________ with the __________ .... Fathers ... bring them up in the training and instruction of the Lord.'*
>
> (Ephesians 5:18; 6:4)

parallels his counsel to parents in Colosse:

> *'Let ______ _________ ____ __________ dwell in you richly .... Fathers, do not embitter your children, or they will become discouraged.'*
>
> (Colossians 3:16, 21)

Moses, in the closing days of his ministry, realised that Israel would not possess their land and influence the nations with God's rule unless each family was saturated with the Word of God:

> *'These ____________________ that I give you today are to be upon your hearts. ____________ them on your children. ________ __________ ________ when you sit at home and when you walk along the road, when you lie down and when you get up.'*
>
> (Deuteronomy 6:6-7)

c. Our goal — foursquare development

Non-Christian experts on children tell us we will have succeeded as parents if our children grow up healthy in *body*, sound in *mind* (and emotions), and well integrated in social *relationships*. That is development in three dimensions only. God's goal for us includes all that, but what else must characterise our family if we would ultimately 'present everyone perfect in Christ' (Colossians 1:28)?

Look at how the boy Jesus displayed God's ideal as he embarked on adolescence:

> *'Jesus grew in ____________ and ____________, and in ____________ with God and men.'*
>
> (Luke 2:52)

Here Dr Luke points out that Jesus' human development occurred not in three dimensions only but in four:

☐ the *physical* ('grew in . . . stature')

☐ the *mental* ('grew in wisdom')

☐ the *social* ('grew in . . . favour with . . . men') and

☐ the *spiritual* ('grew in . . . favour with God')

To be perfect (mature or complete) means:

☐ no part is missing

☐ every part is working

☐ each part is fully developed, and

☐ all parts are harmoniously co-ordinated

So our job isn't through until each grown son and daughter is aglow in *spirit*, sound in *body* and *mind*, and *rightly related* to the redeemed community as well as to their fellow-men and -women. They will be, in general terms, living *for the Lord* (for example, 'Whatever you did for one of the least of these brothers of mine, you did *for me*' — Matthew 25:40).

d. Our reward — ever increasing blessing

1. In the home

What kind of pay can we expect if we rear our families for him? Often in the law and the prophets God guarantees benefits to all who keep his covenant, and lists judgments he will inflict on those who violate it. Several of these affect the family. For instance, through Hosea God warned covenant breakers in northern Israel:

> *'Because you have ignored the law of your God, I also will ignore your children.'*
>
> (Hosea 4:6)

Conversely, the opposite will attend those parents who loyally fulfil their covenant responsibilities: *God will acknowledge their children*.

In Deuteronomy he promises disaster on the family life of apostates:

> *'You will have sons and daughters but you will not keep them, because they will go into captivity.'*
>
> (Deuteronomy 28:41)

What a painful prospect, to lose one's sons and daughters to the bondage of drugs, immorality, covetousness, phobias or heresies! But in complete contrast, under the full covenant blessing *we can keep our children as free persons*.

Through Malachi, the Lord described the ministry of John the Baptist:

> *'He will turn the hearts of the fathers to their children, and the hearts of the children to their fathers; or else I will come and strike the land with a curse.'*
>
> (Malachi 4:6)

Here again the blessing of God is the complete alternative to his curse. He promises not that we can merely keep our families, but that *we will enjoy meaningful heart-to-heart communication with our children*. The prodigal's father kept his older son — but he didn't have his heart's affection (see Luke 15).

2. In society

After his introductory paragraph to the book of Proverbs (1:1-7) Solomon presents twelve sermons to 'my son' in the first nine chapters. In the opening discourse of the series he sets out the advantages of becoming wise (that is, with godly wisdom, not humanism):

> *'Listen, my son, to your father's ____________________ and do not forsake your mother's ______________ . They will be a ____________ to grace your head and a chain to __________ your neck.'*
>
> (Proverbs 1:8-9)

If we raise our children by God's precepts:

☐ *they will turn out to be attractive people*

But that's not all. We will bequeath other social qualities to our sons and daughters by godly upbringing:

☐ *they will be able to discern and choose trustworthy companions and colleagues* and avoid becoming entangled with those who ride roughshod over people for their own gain (Proverbs 1:10-19). And:

☐ *they will be capable of playing a useful role in the life and work of the city* (Proverbs 1:20-33)

In our youth *we* were given the impression that the true church was a ghetto within society. We felt that we were the odd ones out, holding on by the skin of our teeth for the rescue at any moment by the rapture to the clouds.

We have brought up our four children to think very differently. Christians are the normal members of society. That's because they have given heed to wisdom, who makes her presence felt in the fundamental laws of nature (see Proverbs 8:12-36; 3:19-20; 30:24-28) and whose counsel reverberates through the economic laws of honourable commerce in the city (Proverbs 1:20-21). Like Joseph, Moses, Solomon, Daniel and his three friends, they can succeed in their trades and professions to the benefit of society and the glory of God.

3. In the cosmos

God has always put family life on centre stage in all his grand and glorious purposes:

☐ through Adam's family the human race multiplied

☐ through Noah's family humanity was preserved

☐ through Abraham's family all nations on earth will be blessed (see Genesis 22:15-18)

☐ through Messiah's family ('Here am I, and the children God has given me' — Hebrews 2:13) all creation will be restored (Romans 8:18-21)

Cosmic restoration begins at home — your home, our home. Of John the Baptist Jesus said, ' "Elijah comes and will restore all things. But I tell you,

Elijah has already come" .... He was talking ... about John the Baptist' (Matthew 17:11-13).

'Elijah' came in John's ministry, preparing the way of the Lord for his first advent. 'Elijah' has also yet to come to prepare the way for his return. How can we fulfil that preparatory ministry? Just as John did. Did he call fire from heaven? Empty the cemeteries? Convene disarmament conferences? *No!*

> *'See, I will send you the prophet Elijah before that great and dreadful day of the Lord comes. He will turn the hearts of the fathers to their children, and the hearts of the children to their fathers.'*
>
> (Malachi 4:5-6)

It is *good parenting* that prepares the way of the Lord!

2. Practical Implications

Reflect on the purpose of your calling.

We have learnt that our aim as parents is the mature development of each child's potential so that he relates freely with himself, society and God. In the light of this goal, how should we practise that oft-recited but largely misunderstood verse from Proverbs about child-rearing?

> *'Train a child in the way he should go, and when he is old he will not turn from it.'*
>
> (Proverbs 22:6)

This is generally quoted as if it meant: cram enough Bible into your child's head and when he grows up he will not become an agnostic or atheist, an alcoholic or an adulterer. However, not a few who had religion imposed on them as children have turned from God as adults.

What does the verse *actually* say?

a. Channel his talents creatively

'Train up a child . . . in keeping with his individual gift or bent' (Amp), 'for his proper trade' (Moffatt). This translation accords with Paul's counsel to fathers:

> *'Do not embitter your children, or they will become discouraged.'*
>
> (Colossians 3:21)

In former generations, for instance, left-handed children were *not* trained in their natural tendency but forced to use their right hands, as a result of which some became dyslexic or developed a stammer.

J.A. Hadfield defines maturation as 'the development of innate potentialities in ordered sequence'. You can only 'e-ducate' (Latin, 'lead out') what is already within; you can't train a pig to sing — he doesn't have that talent in him!

b. Curb his tendency towards chaos

Another interpretation of this verse could be: 'Hedge in a child upon the mouth (that is, the beginning) of his way.' Literally 'make it narrow for a child'; hedge him in, as a cowboy corrals cattle; restrict his self-will, because folly is bound up in his heart (Proverbs 22:15). In this way you will guard his soul (v5).

One tendency needing control is *aggression*. This strong natural drive needs to be controlled in adults as well as children. If an infant is allowed to continue aggressive crying he becomes afraid of the monster of his own anger, which leads ultimately to some measure of self-rejection and guilt.

Which view of this verse is right? Since the Hebrew is flexible we will accept both! We must *restrain* and *train*; discipline must *correct* and *direct*.

But in addition to good potential abilities that we must *draw forth*, and sinful potentialities that we must *hold back*, there is a fundamental ingredient we must constantly *put in* to each child:

c. Communicate God's unconditional love

The three vital ingredients in training up a child can be represented by an equilateral triangle. The diagrams show how the three ingredients need to be kept in balance, and what happens if one ingredient is out of proportion.

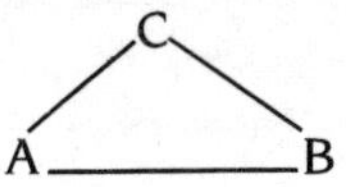

Base AB = unconditional love (put in)
Side AC = discipline (hold back)
Side BC = freedom (draw forth)

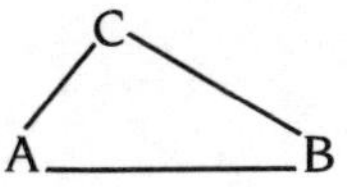

We do not spoil a child by too much love. It isn't possible to overdose him with love. Rather, a child is spoilt by too little discipline (and the corresponding excess license — he becomes overwhelmed with the need to make too many personal choices).

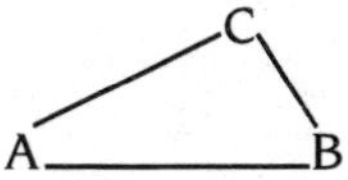

He can also become disturbed by too harsh a regime of discipline (and the resulting restriction of freedom).

Inconsistent discipline will create problems, too. Birth was an enormous trauma to the baby — through a restrictive passageway from the warmth of his mother's body where he had enjoyed the reassuring drumbeat of her heart, into a strange big world where he often feels brutal hunger pangs and an uncomfortable rear-end. He often finds himself torn between the two strong opposing desires:

☐ to revert to the security of the womb

☐ to reach out to the novelty of the world

In his first couple of years mother provides for both these basic needs, granting him a rich foundational experience of the love of God.

It is not far-fetched to say that from mother he forms his first understanding of God as *immanent* (God-with-us), because in those first two years he is unaware that he and mother are two distinct people. The God who became incarnate at Bethlehem is pleased to reveal the supernatural via the natural: 'the spiritual did not come first, but the natural, and after that the spiritual' (1 Corinthians 15:46).

The Lord's Supper, the nourishing of our spirits on his love by eating his flesh and drinking his blood, is a perfect parallel to the infant's feeding off his mother and experiencing her love.

Father comes into the infant's reckoning between age two and five. From him he begins to experience God as *transcendent* (Dad is always 'other'); he appears to have unlimited freedom and power ('my dad can do everything'). It broadens the child's experience of the grandeur of God's love.

****

LESSON 1

A Rewarding Responsibility

True or False

1. T F Secular books on raising children are completely unreliable because they do not quote the Bible.

2. T F To become a disciple of Jesus he says we must hate our children (Luke 14:26). This statement refers to his ownership of them and to our stewardship of them as parents.

3. T F God's purpose for parents was expressed in what Pharaoh's daughter said to Moses' mother: 'Take this baby and nurse him for me, and I will pay you.'

4. T F Moses tells us fathers and mothers in Deuteronomy 6 to keep God's commandments in our hearts but only refer to them in passing to our children.

5. T F The spiritual dimension of our children's development involves their growing in favour with God. Non-Christian experts on parenthood usually confine their comments to the other three areas of development: body, mind and relationships.

6. T F If we live by the covenant, Scripture promises only that we will not lose our children. A continuing open relationship with them is a bonus.

7. T F We must instil into our children that the church will always be on the defensive in society.

8. T F Godly home life contributes to society's improvement.

9. T F Children are never spoiled by too much love but by bad discipline.

Group Discussion

1. Talk over the differences it will make (or has already made) when we really *see* that parenthood is a divine stewardship.

2. Testify to one another of the covenant blessings you have enjoyed since you first set out to do things God's way. Tell from your own experience (or observation) of family problems due to disobeying or ignoring God's Word.

3. Remind each other of godly people who have benefited society in practical ways because of their faith.

4. Discuss that it is impossible to show too much love to your children: *that* will never spoil them. How can we show God's love in the infant's formative years?

Personal Assignment

1. Monitor yourself for a whole week on *how* you speak and listen to your children. Ask yourself continually: 'Do I really believe they are the King's kids?'

2. As day by day you take God's commandments to heart for yourself, begin to 'talk about them' to your children as you sit or walk, as you put them to bed or wake them up for school.

3. Tell the children repeatedly that as King's kids they are special, that they can benefit their friends, school class, team, etc.

4. Ask the Lord to make you aware of:

   a. some talent in each child you can train

   b. any tendency you must take steps to restrain

   c. meaningful ways to communicate his love to each child individually

True or False

1.F 2.T 3.T 4.F 5.T 6.F 7.F 8.T 9.T

Attitudes and Atmosphere

1. The Key to World Dominion

In lesson 1 we learned that godly home life has beneficial repercussions in society and prepares the way of the Lord for the restoration of the whole cosmos.

Originally God planned to rule the world from his home in Eden through Adam and his bride (Genesis 1 — 2). He intends to govern the universe through Jesus — the last Adam — and his bride — the church — from his new home, the garden city, new Jerusalem (Revelation 21 — 22).

God made man in his own image to rule creation by breathing into his nostrils the *spirit* of life (Genesis 2:7 literally). It is from a person's spirit that attitudes and motivations spring:

> ' *The word of God . . . . penetrates even to dividing soul and* __________ *. . . it judges the thoughts and* ________________ *of the heart.'*
>
> (Hebrews 4:12)

An unhealthy state of spirit generates bad attitudes that do not produce dominion but defeat.

a. Progressive rule

Only when a parent has '*control over his spirit*' (Proverbs 25:28 NASB), or 'self-control' (NIV) can he (or she):

- ☐ '*manage his own family well* and see that his children obey him with proper respect' (1 Timothy 3:5); and thus qualify as:
- ☐ be an 'overseer' (1 Timothy 3:2) '*who directs the affairs of the church well*' (1 Timothy 5:17)

Only from such a 'home', a rightly ordered church filled with his presence, can God *govern the powers of darkness* through his people: 'The Lord will extend your mighty sceptre from Zion; you will rule in the midst of your enemies. Your troops will be willing on your day of battle' (Psalm 110:2-3)

b. The influence of attitude

It is all too easy for us parents to assume we can make successes of our children by forceful words and blustering actions. We will succeed when our words and actions are the fruit of a right attitude. Even very young children perceive when our attitudes contradict our speech and actions.

Child psychologist J.A. Hadfield, during a week's holiday by the sea, cast a professional eye over two fathers with their four-year-old sons. To get into the sea, bathers had to cross an area of pebbles barefoot. Mr A told his boy, 'Of course it doesn't hurt,' but his son still moaned about this short walk every day because he saw the unconfessed pain on his dad's face. Mr B admitted, 'Sure it hurts, but take my hand and we'll go together,' and never again did his boy complain!

c. Assess your attitudes

Repeatedly in Psalm 51 David, in his desire to be utterly honest with himself before the Lord following his gross sins of adultery and murder-by-proxy, refers to his spirit or inner parts (see v6, 10-12, 17). Using this prayer of his, let us each ask ourselves: What is *my* attitude as a parent?

1. Is it a vacillating attitude?

God desires a *true* and *wise* spirit:

> *'Surely you desire __________ in the _________ parts; you teach me ____________ in the __________ place?'*
>
> (Psalm 51:6)

The Hebrew for truth is like the old English word in the traditional wedding vow: 'plight thee my *troth*' — in other words, loyalty, faithfulness. It's not the military discipline of the prodigal's brother ('All these years I've been slaving for you' — what an attitude!), but the warm dependability of the prodigal's father.

Attitudes and Atmosphere

It is wise to practise truth, and folly to behave in inconsistent ways for that only breeds insecurity in a child:

☐ Do I keep my promises?

☐ Do I resolve disputes fairly?

☐ Do I resist manipulation by the family 'cutie' and the family bully?

2. *Is it an abdicating attitude?*

'Renew a ________________ __________ within me.'

(Psalm 51:10)

☐ Do I opt out of family decision-making?

☐ Do I fail to intervene when there are difficulties at school?

☐ Do I get involved in my teenagers' career choices?

3. *Is it a manipulative attitude?*

'Grant me a ________________ __________, to sustain me.'

(Psalm 51:12)

☐ Do I always get my own way in family discussions about how we will spend our free time and holidays?

☐ Do we only watch *my* favourite TV programme?

☐ Do I always force chores on the children because I am not prepared to inconvenience myself?

4. *Is it a domineering attitude?*

'The sacrifices of God are a __________ __________; a broken and ________________ __________, O God, you will not despise.'

(Psalm 51:17)

☐ Am I harsh and proud?

☐ Can I empathise with the children in their disappointments, fears and frustrations?

Take time to *ask God*: 'Search me, O God, and know my heart' (Psalm 139:23).

Ask your spouse: 'Listen to whatever Sarah tells you' (Genesis 21:12).

Ask your children: 'Come now, let us reason together' (Isaiah 1:18).

Ask your spiritual shepherd: 'If there is iniquity in me,' said David to Jonathan, 'put me to death yourself' (1 Samuel 20:8).

2. Parents' Attitudes

a. To your own parents

What is your attitude to your own parents — whether they are still alive or are now dead? Have you cut the invisible psychological umbilical cord of 'mother's apron-strings' or do her emotions domineer your thinking still?

Have you forgiven your parents for painful incidents or unprofitable attitudes towards you in childhood, or do you still harbour grudges and nurse resentment towards them?

Do you allow grandparents to lower standards and break established rules of discipline (such as bedtimes, no sweets between meals)? If not, you need to sit down with them and explain the situation respectfully but firmly.

b. To one another

What is your attitude towards each other — whether still together, divorced or widowed?

For details on how to argue things through to a purposeful conclusion we refer you to lesson 5 in our other School of the Word, *Fulfilment in Marriage* (Harvestime).

Good attitude is the essential ingredient in resolving all differences. Raising a complaint against one's spouse need not be the same as blaming him or her. We believe it is better for the children to see that you *can* disagree and resolve your differences than that you should pretend 'never to argue in front of the kids'.

One such mother of two infants got an eye-opener one day when she tried to stop them quarrelling and was given the explanation by her five-year-old daughter, pointing at her three-year-old brother, 'He started it. He called me "darling" first!'

c. To yourself

Parenting at times can be an exhilaratingly fulfilling occupation. More often it is just plain flat and very routine; but now and again it can prove to be very frustrating — the new baby's three-month colic that deprives us of sleep; the missing shoes just as we are all bundling into the car for a deadline appointment; the mum housebound for days on end with a hyperactive tribe in quarantine with measles; the teenager who treats 'chez nous' as a mere café and doss-house. At such times it is vital not to slip into a Cinderella mentality, 'Poor old me.'

James prescribes the perfect cure for this diseased attitude — the word of truth about ourselves:

> *'Every good and perfect gift is from above, coming down from the __________ of the heavenly lights, who does ______ ____________ like shifting shadows.*
>
> *'He__________ to give us birth through the* **word** *of truth, that we might be a kind of firstfruits of all he created . . . .*
>
> *'Humbly accept the* **word** *planted in you, which can________ you.*
>
> *'Do not merely ____________ to the* **word***, and so deceive yourselves. Do what it says. Anyone who ____________ to the* **word** *but does not do what it says is like a man who looks at his face in a mirror and, after looking at himself, goes away and immediately forgets what he looks like. But the man who looks intently into the perfect law that __________ ____________, and continues to do this, not forgetting what he ______ __________, but doing it — he will be blessed in what he does.'*
>
> (James 1:17-25)

Reread those missing and emphasised words. We have a *Father* who *chose* to give us birth (so we have his nature) by means of his *Word*, and doesn't ever *change* his mind; let us listen attentively to that law of his which gives us *freedom*, and start to act on what it says to us and it will *save* us — make us whole persons.

d. To each child

Our relationship to our children should be that of friendship, not frenzy! Friendship does not require that the partners be equals. Abraham was a friend of God and the twelve apostles were friends of their Lord and Master. Our children relate to us without an economic contract — that's a good basis for real friendship.

We can monitor our attitude by its fruits: a good atmosphere and wholesome activities.

1. Atmosphere

A good home atmosphere radiates love and encouragement, openness and trust, respect and discipline, authority and freedom for growth.

Let's elaborate on a couple of these ingredients.

i. Unconditional love

No child of ours should ever feel unwanted ('I wish we'd never had you'), that he is a target of our jealousy ('I'm your husband but you give more attention to that child than to me') or that he must earn our acceptance. Our heavenly Father's communication to his only begotten Son demonstrates the correct perspective in parenthood. At his baptism God tore heaven open (Mark 1:10) to tell him:

> *'You are my Son, whom I love; with you I am well pleased.'*
>
> (Mark 1:11)

☐ *Show acceptance of his person before you*

☐ *Speak approval of his performance*

Even the new baby needs to have his being affirmed ('You are') before his behaviour is assessed. Relationship is not based on performance — Jesus had not worked a single miracle at this stage.

The second half of God's statement in Mark 1:11 probably refers to Jesus' activities; throughout Scripture divine pleasure and displeasure seems always to be God's response to righteous or unrighteous behaviour (e.g. 2 Samuel 11:27; Haggai 1:8; John 8:29; 1 Corinthians 10:5).

As the child grows up he is able more and more to motivate himself, accept goals and congratulate himself on fulfilling those aims. Then we can:

☐ *Share in his achievements* 'Father . . . . I have brought you glory on earth by completing the work you gave me to do' (John 17:1, 4)

What does all this mean in everyday life?

☐ Acceptance

Love your child for who he is, not for what he has done.

Let *each* child be your *favourite* (and tell him so) for some *personal asset* (i.e. being) such as: 'This is my favourite youngest and this my favourite oldest; you are my special five-year-old, or my only adopted daughter'; not for some *performance* (i.e. behaviour) such as 'best at spelling; great on the guitar; smiles the most; best behaved; most polite; tidiest'. If you base your love on performance there is always the risk to his status when he fails to achieve or another in the family becomes equally capable at it.

Love him exactly the same when he has failed. He can't alter who he is but he can change his behaviour.

☐ Demonstration of your love

If he is unaware of his acceptance, your love is ineffectual.

- By touch and words, for example tuck him up in bed even when he is a bit older
- Make allowance for her outbursts of frustration. ('You don't love me' and 'I hate you' are cries for love)
- Don't correct her in front of her friends
- Safeguard him against the intrusion of his siblings
- Don't demand that he perform before guests, unless he volunteers

– Be at home to welcome her back from school

– Boast of her when she has done nothing special

– Leave a thoughtful note when you will not be at home

☐ Praise and criticism

– Praise her efforts, not her looks, brains or cuteness (flattery is a form of *rejection* — Proverbs 26:28; also 28:23; 29:5)

– Praise the specific. When told every time, 'That's a good picture', the seven-year-old was heard to ask his friend, 'What do you have to do around here to paint a *bad* picture?' If you say: 'That's a good boy,' he is confused if he felt in a nasty mood when he did his good deed; rather, 'That was kind of you to lend your bike to Michael.'

– Remember, direct sunlight tends to dazzle, so measure your praise soberly

– Affirm your love before you offer advice or criticism (like Jesus and the woman of Sychar)

– Criticise her actions and attitudes, not her person: 'You spilt the milk, now mop it up'; not 'You great clumsy oaf!'

– Avoid sarcasm: 'Were you born on a raft in mid-ocean? Shut the door!'

– Don't over-explain: 'Because I said so' is sufficient for most commands.

– Verbalise your feelings: 'I'm annoyed,' so that he doesn't take your anger as a cancellation of your love.

– Speak faith, not doubts and fears.

ii. Respect

A kingdom home is one in which:

☐ God is given the pre-eminence

☐ Father and mother love each other

☐ Rules are based on good example

☐ Attractive decor is used

☐ Good health habits are practised

☐ Information is given on moral values

☐ Right to privacy is observed

☐ Everyone is taken seriously: time, attention and an attempt to understand each other

☐ Fun and good humour abound

2. Activities

Don't crowd him. Give him scope to develop a healthy life of his own. He can only freely say yes when he is able to say no. Even a baby needs space. Beware of 'smother love'.

Seeing our grandson climb up and down stairs unaided just after his first birthday was a real education. And one school we read about had a big tree in its backyard that any child was allowed to climb unassisted, the philosophy being that if he can get to any branch he can get back down again. One seven-year-old improved his mathematics dramatically from the day he got up to the first branch and down again. Mothers never knew of its use for years until one child was seen from the front of the school above the level of the school roof in the topmost branch!

The bully is often a bored under-achiever; he needs to be provided with equipment and the offer of a choice of activities. Even newborn babies love intellectual stimulation.

3. The family honesty game

Each member writes down privately his *many* appreciations but only one grievance concerning each of the others, and father raises the points *with great discretion*.

4. The family conference table

☐ Select the place and time: the lounge, around the coffee table at 6.30

☐ State the purpose: to confer (not argue); to forgive and ask for help (not to bully); to find answers

☐ Spell out procedure: if anyone raises his voice, interrupts or acts unhelpfully, any other member can stand in silent protest

3. The Child's Attitudes

a. To himself

His view of himself is largely the product of what others have told him in his first five to ten years of life – like that party game when a famous name is pinned to your back and you have to find out who you are by how people answer your questions! Let us *work* at conveying to him his self-worth.

1. God thinks he is wonderful

He made him wonderful (Psalm 139:13-16), redeemed him with the blood of his Son (1 Peter 1:18-19) and adopted him as a co-heir with Jesus (Romans 8:14-17).

2. Show him that you think he is wonderful

☐ Hear his opinions and grievances even if you cannot endorse them

☐ Don't keep interrupting her

☐ Feed back to him what you *think* he is saying

☐ Be open to change your opinions on non-essentials

☐ When you disagree, do so pleasantly

☐ Don't ridicule her, nor let others do so

☐ Give each child individual time (e.g. a 'Daddy Ticket' for his birthday giving him an event of his choice with his father); remember, 'fair is not necessarily equal'.

☐ Keep her secrets

☐ Communicate warm emotions, not just cold facts

3. Help him verbalise his feelings

We used to have great fun talking to our four when they were little about 'warm fuzzies' (good feelings) and 'cold pricklies' (such as upsets and anxieties). We would play: 'Look at me with a cold prickly; watch my face for a warm fuzzy.'

Strong emotions that cause the memory to freeze up (as in exams) can throw our view of situations out of perspective (such as panic or bullying). Helping your child to speak about how he feels provides him with an emotional safety valve and will help him to control strong reactions.

4. Let him know you understand how he feels

☐ 'Your brother got a present. It's *his* birthday. But I love you, too'

☐ 'You got all of your sums wrong today. Did that make you feel stupid? When *I'm* worried *I* also forget how to count correctly!'

☐ 'He called you a liar. Did that make you feel angry with him?'

☐ As you hold the three-year-old in your arms, struggling and kicking because he wants to stay on the swings when you are about to be late for lunch: 'I know you feel like killing me. But we'll both make Mum sad if lunch is spoilt'

b. To his parents

1. Obedience

We will show in lesson 5 how to begin to produce obedience in a young child.

2. Respect

> *'Children, ________ your parents in the Lord, for this is right. ____________ your father and mother.'*
>
> (Ephesians 6:1-2)

You can make a child obey by force, punishment or reward. But you cannot make him honour you; you must earn that respect. Children are, in fact, responders. The Bible hints at this: the New Testament description of John the Baptist's ministry only quotes the first half of his job description from four hundred years before in the Old Testament:

> *'Elijah . . . will turn the hearts of the fathers to their children, and the hearts of the children to their fathers.'*
>
> (Malachi 4:5-6)

Zechariah, John's father, seems to imply that if fathers act honourably their children's hearts *will* turn towards them (see Luke 1:17).

c. To brothers and sisters

So much will depend on how parents oversee their children's interaction, especially when a new baby arrives while the previous child is still young (see lesson 4). We will fail if we try to love each child equally to prevent rivalry and jealousy. Instead we should love each child extremely and totally!

d. To life

We don't know who first said it but it sums up our job: 'The best thing parents can do for their children is to give them roots and wings' — security and freedom.

Build his confidence. A child who lacks confidence can miss so many of the best things in childhood or later life, such as making friends and trying new experiences.

☐ Listen sympathetically: don't sweep problems under the carpet

☐ Give him information about what will happen

☐ Focus on what he will enjoy and feel comfortable about

☐ Be specific with your warnings: not, 'Be careful. Can you manage?' but, 'Don't put your fingers near the blade'

☐ Don't thrust him suddenly into lots of new experiences; stay with him till he weighs things up

☐ Never tease or nag him about his shyness

☐ Rehearse new situations in advance using role play

☐ Replace his memory of failures with compensating good experiences

LESSON 2

Attitudes and Atmosphere

True or False

1. T F Attitudes are products of a person's spirit.
2. T F Right attitudes are vital to our reigning in life.
3. T F It is essential for a parent to exert a domineering spirit in order to keep his family in order.
4. T F Grudges towards our own parents for childhood hurts will adversely affect our task as parents.
5. T F A wife should never voice complaints to her husband because that is the same as blaming him.
6. T F The word of truth about ourselves will help us form a good self image.
7. T F Technically it is an impossible dream to want to be a friend of our children.
8. T F Approving a child's performance is more important than accepting his person.
9. T F It is possible to treat each child as the favourite.
10. T F Young children do not have a right to privacy — it only breeds cunning and secrecy in later life.
11. T F Good parent/child communications develop naturally and cannot be learned.
12. T F If you ever change your opinion at your child's suggestion you will forfeit his respect.
13. T F To teach a child how to verbalise his feelings gives him an emotional safety valve and will help him to control strong reactions.

14. T F You can improve a child's confidence by rehearsing a new challenge in advance.

Group Discussion

1. Talk together from experience and observation of how attitudes to one's own parents affects our attitudes to our children.
2. Discuss unconditional love.
3. Exchange practical ideas for improving your child's self-image and confidence.

Personal Assignment

1. Check out your own spirit in terms of Psalm 51. Make all necessary adjustments.
2. Assess your attitudes to:
    a. yourself
    b. your parents
    c. your spouse
    d. each of your children
3. Put into practice the things you have learnt in this lesson about creating a good home atmosphere.
4. Try the honesty game.
5. Conduct a session of family conference.

True or False

1.T 2.T 3.F 4.T 5.F 6.T 7.F 8.F 9.T 10.T 11.F 12.F 13.T 14.T

LESSON 3

The Forming of a Person

1. Contributing Factors

a. Constitutional ingredients

A gardener planting out a seedling must know the nature of the young piece of vegetation. If it is a bean sprout he knows he will never gather raspberries from its adult branches! The purpose of this lesson is to help us to get to know the make-up of each of our offspring.

Good Housekeeping magazine told how nineteen-year-old Bobby Shafran, adopted as a baby, discovered that he had an identical twin studying at the same college. Eddy Galland, also adopted, shared his birthday and birth place. When their story broke in the newspapers, David Kellman, a student at Queens College, New York, telephoned to say that he must be their triplet brother! They were history's first recorded instance of the reunion of identical triplets who had been separated at birth.

They had been raised in quite different environments — Bobby's father was a doctor whose wife worked in the legal profession; the Kellmans ran a wholesale houseware business; Mr Galland was a teacher and his wife an executive secretary with a love of cooking.

Yet the boys discovered that they shared many identical characteristics: each had a high I.Q., smoked the same brand of cigarette, preferred older girls, liked Italian food, participated in wrestling and specialised in the same range of holds, often dreamed he had a brother who looked just like him, and got psychiatric help at sixteen but rejected the diagnosis that his emotional problems stemmed from his adoption in infancy!

Not only are physical features predetermined in the genes of the original fertilised ovum in the womb — eye colour, sporting and musical talent, etc.

— but even future ministry is God-ordained before the baby draws his first breath. God told Jeremiah:

> *'Before I formed you in the womb I knew you, before you were born I______ you________ ; I appointed you as a____________ to the nations.'*
>
> (Jeremiah 1:5)

Parents, therefore, must operate within the child's God-given constitution: 'Train up a child . . . in keeping with his individual gift or bent' (Proverbs 22:6 Amp).

b. Conditional influences

Although the child cannot change his eye colour from dark brown to bright blue, it is not a matter of fate that he must read certain books with those eyes. He could have the potential to become an operatic tenor but end up yelling punk rock!

When those triplet brothers met they were training for very different careers — each in a field in which *one of his parents* was already deeply involved: Bobby hoped to qualify as a doctor, Eddy as a catering manager and David as a businessman.

So, what are a child's main conditioning influences?

1. The nuclear family

Some years ago the humanistic philosophy of sociology started to invade the churches, belittling the nuclear family (that is, father, mother and the children) and advocating the merits of communal living. Of course, in many African and Oriental cultures the extended family is the norm. But God made it plain from the beginning that:

> *'A man shall __________ his ____________ and ____________ and be __________ ____ his ________ .'*
>
> (Genesis 2:24)

The walls of family order should be securely built and kept in good repair. Children feel safer with clearly defined boundaries. There can be tragic long-term effects, for example, if Grandma's influence is allowed to replace that of the working mother. And we always put limits on the disciplinary rights of our part-time babysitters to prevent resentment arising in our youngsters.

2. Birth order

One's place in the family birth order has no inescapable influence, but it can help to explain why each child develops certain *tendencies*. These trends will normally occur only if the age gaps are reasonably small. In general:

☐ the first-born attempts to conquer the world

☐ the second-born aims to live in harmony with the world

☐ the third-born expects to encounter the world adventurously

The *first-born* tends to be conservative, serious, adult-oriented, loyal and self-sufficient (e.g. Abraham), even legalistic (e.g. the prodigal's brother). He can feel exploited, and jealous of the series of new babies who dethroned him (e.g. Cain).

The *second-born* can be lazy and selfish, unwilling to compete in areas already claimed by the first-born. He can be placid (like Jacob) or rebellious (like the prodigal) and will usually need a pace-setter in life.

The *third-born* can be a loner, a daydreamer (e.g. Moses) who also accepts forgiveness readily.

The *last-born* may withdraw, lack self-confidence because the older children always 'babied' him (e.g. Gideon), and can be a tell-tale (like Joseph) who wants a special friend, despite the houseful of siblings! He may also like to challenge opponents stronger than himself at great personal risk (e.g. David and Gideon).

The *only* child can be imperious and manipulative, an individualist because of unmitigated 'smother love' (e.g. Samson). He is likely to be achievement-oriented and have difficulty making friends (e.g. Isaac) or become a selfless martyr (e.g. John the Baptist).

3. Step-relatives

The conditioning influence of step-relatives is an all-too-common feature of our generation — mainly the product of divorce and remarriage. A major problem to watch is the potential disunity between mother and father ('Why is *he* correcting *my* daughter?'). And rivalry can arise if children *of the same age* become step-brothers/sisters — a situation that foster agencies and adoption societies try to avoid.

The story of Isaac and Rebekah and their twin sons (Genesis 24 — 25) can teach us what to avoid (even though they were not step-relatives): *favouritism, rivalry* and *secret manipulation*. We advise that, when children are brought into a new marriage, pastoral care be sought, especially in the early years of the marital merger. Learn to talk openly about the pressures you each feel, and to speak out your faith in God's grace to get things right.

4. The tribe

Although the Bible discourages the extended family commune, it often refers to the blessing of enjoying one's children's children. Aunts and uncles, as well as grandparents, have a valuable contribution to the forming of the child's life, provided they do not undermine the parents' vital role. Timothy's flame of faith was lit by his grandmother, Lois, and stoked up by his mother, Eunice (2 Timothy 1:5).

5. The church

Our own children not only 'attended church' regularly but throughout their formative years had the church attend them — a constant flood of godly 'aunties' and 'uncles' brought to them the fun and fellowship of faith.

Because Jacob stopped short of Bethel (meaning 'the house of God') in order to better himself by swapping his pilgrim's tent for a settler's house in Shechem, his daughter lost her virginity, whereupon her blood brothers proceeded to disgrace the family name (see Genesis 31:13; 34:1-31). We have observed many Christians who have compromised their convictions about the church in order to gain worldly promotion. Frequently their kids have lost out spiritually, sometimes in very serious ways.

Thankfully, Jacob eventually not only *got to* the house of God (Genesis 35) but his family truly *became* the house of God — he was the only patriarch to have a totally united family around him in his sunset years, all of them committed to the Lord!

6. Society

We need to be alert to the influences of the neighbourhood, the school and the gang. When we have the power of choice about where to live and which school to use, let us exercise that right.

But we need not run scared about the world's influence, for greater is he who is in us than he who is in the world. Let's practise situational teaching every time we are aware of unrighteousness or lack of wisdom in the society in which our children live; we cannot stop the world and get off, but we can maintain a kingdom atmosphere, even in alien circumstances.

c. Personal intentions

We began this chapter by considering the factors of *heredity* and *environment* as they moulded triplet brothers. But there is a third factor — *the child's own responses*.

When we were teenagers we knew triplet brothers, though in this instance they were brought up together. They too thought alike and responded identically to most events in life. If they were in three different places when one suddenly developed certain medical symptoms, the other two would experience them at the same time.

In spiritual things, however, it was different. Each brother came under conviction of sin and yielded his life to Christ quite separately and individually, clearly indicating that conviction of sin is a question neither of 'nature' (heredity) nor of 'nurture' (environment), since all three lads heard the same preaching at their local chapel. Conviction of sin is a supernatural work of the Holy Spirit, overruling both nature and nurture, and cannot be put down to merely psychological factors.

To summarise this section of our study:

1. In part the child is made

His *temperament*, being derived from heredity (in his genes), is *constitutional*. This is the picture-frame within which the masterpiece of character will be painted. It is fixed, so our parental contribution here is zero.

2. In part he is being made

His *disposition* is being formed by his environment — parents, brothers and sisters, neighbours, school supply of 'paints and brushes', etc. These are *conditional*. He may be musical by nature, but whether he becomes a pianist or a guitarist may depend on the availability of a piano. In this area we *can* exercise substantial influence.

3. In part he makes himself

His *character* ultimately depends on his own responses, aims, purposes and ideals — and these are *chosen by him*. His choices can be influenced by parental example, instruction and prayer.

2. Ages and Stages

In his first letter, the apostle John refers to phases of spiritual growth in terms of stages of natural development:

> *'I write to you, dear ____________, because your sins have been forgiven on account of his name. I write to you, __________, because you have known him who is from the beginning. I write to you, _____________, because you have overcome the evil one. I write to you, dear ____________, because you have known the Father. I write to you, __________, because you have known him who is from the beginning. I write to you, _____________, because you are strong, and the word of God lives in you, and you have overcome the evil one.'*
>
> (1 John 2:12-14)

Certain new characteristics predominate at each successive stage of a child's growth, adding to those remaining from earlier stages:

The healthy *infant*:

☐ recognises the father

☐ receives his forgiveness

A healthy natural baby needs the security of knowing to whom he belongs, and that he is accepted and loved by them.

The healthy *youth*:

☐ internalises the Word

☐ conquers the wicked one

The well-developed adolescent can think soundly for himself and needs a cause to fight for.

A healthy *father* (not just 'adult'):

☐ experiences the Lord (who in 1 John 1:1-3 is *the* life of the ages)

☐ extends his life — by the reproduction of spiritual children into whom he pours his own spiritual life for their upbringing

In the formation of a person, what are the distinct stages and their main features?

a. Infancy (birth to four years)

0-1 he is *physically dependent*

1-2 still dependent but also invading his environment

2½-4 *emotionally dependent*, being suggestible to mother's reactions of approval or disapproval, but also assertive (frustration tantrums can be common)

b. Childhood (5 to 11+ years)

5-7 a transition phase (when he loses his 'milk teeth'). A time of marked individuality — 'primary adolescence'

8-11+ *socially dependent* on companions — 'primitive man'

c. Adolescence (12 to 18 years)

12-15 another transition: *socially dependent* — gang loyalty

16-18 *dependent on ideals*: hero-objects of the same sex; love-objects of the opposite sex

d. Adulthood (18 onwards)

18-21 yet another transition into full adulthood — by which time we hope he is mature

From these simple observations of the human race we note that, whereas animals grow up in a straight line of development, the 'man cub' tends, at certain stages, to display a pattern of emotional reversion: the 8-12 phase resembles an early adulthood ('primitive man'), yet is followed at 12-15 by more of the assertiveness/tantrums characteristic of the 2½-4 stage, as well as the individualism of the 5-7 stage.

e. What then is maturity?

It includes at least two vital ingredients: *continuity* and *development*.

1. Continuity

As we noted about the stages of spiritual growth in 1 John 2:12-14, a 'father' still knows the heavenly Father and his forgiveness, as the infant does, and *continues* to assimilate God's Word and to use it in the defeat of the devil, as the 'young man' does.

We listened with sadness to a radio interview with a one-time BBC producer whose powers of recall lasted for less than ten minutes, due to a brain-cell wasting disease. He often crossed out the previous day's entries in his personal diary, being convinced he must have made up those accounts of what were by then forgotten events. Without a settled memory of our past we cannot truly grow up — good foundations in childhood are vital in the forming of a mature person.

2. Development

From the above ages-and-stages notes you will observe that *development* includes a shifting of the child's dependence from external events to internal images.

The new baby, when awake, needs a lot of physical contact with his mother. The toddler requires this less frequently but still needs her presence to give him an atmosphere of peace and love. The child at school can happily spend long hours away from her actual presence because he has developed a deep-seated internal image of her love and faith — a bit like taking your driving test, when your faithful instructor is no longer beside you in the car but his oft-repeated comments live on in your mind.

The developing child continues to be a dependent person, however, drawing first on gang approval and later on hero-worship and some grand ideal.

And what about the mature adult — should we conclude that he has achieved true independence? Strictly speaking, no. Although he is able to think for himself and be 'self-contained' in whatever circumstances he finds himself (the literal meaning of 'content' in Philippians 4:12), still the mature Christian testifies, 'I can do everything through *him* who gives me strength' (Philippians 4:13). He operates from a clear conscience, 'conscience' literally meaning 'co-knowledge' (con-science) — his knowledge of life is shared with *the Other* within; he still depends totally on the grace of God and as a result can stand on his own two feet.

3. Development in Four Dimensions

To return to the gardening analogy with which we began this lesson, we may say that our children will develop:

- ☐ *Spiritually* by putting down strong roots into God's truth and opening their leaves to the sunshine of God's love and the atmosphere of his presence
- ☐ *Physically* like a tree's strong trunk and branch system
- ☐ *Mentally* with the rising sap of enquiry and thought
- ☐ *Socially* as they develop blossom and fruit that attracts others to them

We are stewards of God's little ones. While mother may plant and father may water, it is God who gives the growth. But our lack of planting and watering would most certainly hinder growth in each of these vital dimensions.

LESSON 3

The Forming of a Person

True or False

1. T F The nuclear family (father, mother and children) is of little importance in today's society.
2. T F Birth order within the family can influence a person's disposition.
3. T F First-born children often tend to be both loyal and legalistic.
4. T F Favouritism, jealousy and manipulation will never arise among step-children in a Christian home.
5. T F Grandparents cannot influence their children's children.
6. T F Parents who are actively committed to their local church community can expect their children to benefit thereby.
7. T F The child's own choices determine his character.
8. T F Normal healthy children develop in a straight, steady line towards adulthood, just as animals do.
9. T F Dependence is an essential feature of being human.
10. T F As a child develops through various age brackets his focus of dependence shifts.

Group Discussion

1. Share together your real life observations that cast light on the 'nature versus nurture' debate: What characteristics in your children are inborn and inherited? What influences for change do school, TV, friends, church, etc. have upon them?
2. Discuss the ways in which your children's dispositions have been moulded by their position in the family order. Which of these attitudes need to be redressed? How can you go about changing them?

3. Talk about the special problems of step-children and step-parents and suggest practical ways of resolving them.

Personal Assignment

1. Carefully assess each of your children in terms of:

   a. God-given abilities

   b. temperament

   c. disposition (attitudes)

   d. ages and stages

   e. how they are influenced by older, younger or twin brothers or sisters, or lack of any

   In the light of your observations seek God for individual ways to develop each child.

True or False

1.F 2.T 3.T 4.F 5.F 6.T 7.T 8.F 9.T 10.T

Deliverance and Development

1. Development

What is a child? Just a cute living toy? Not in the opinion of his older brothers and sisters! He is little, inexperienced (but not innocent) and often clumsy, yet capable of serious enquiry and experiment.

a. Weaning

We have already noted his inborn opposing urges: on the one hand to revert to the safety of the womb but on the other to reach out to the challenge of the world. As parents, therefore, we must provide both *security* and *stimulus*. Also we must realise that in the process of his development he undergoes repeatedly the crisis of weaning — leaving behind some aspect of his security in his desire to embrace novelty.

The psalmist testified:

> *'I have stilled and quietened my soul; like a weaned child with its __________, like a __________ __________ is my __________ __________ me.'*
>
> (Psalm 131:2)

Paul described his spiritual progress as:

> *'__________________ what is behind and ______________ ______________ what is ahead, I __________ ____ towards the goal to win the prize for which God has called me ____________________ in Christ Jesus.'*
>
> (Philippians 3:13-14)

Birth is an event as traumatic as Adam and Eve's expulsion from Eden into the great outside world which they were to conquer. For a while, baby enjoys a symbiotic union (mutually beneficial dependence) with mother as he is nourished at her breast. Then weaning releases him from this dependence on mother's milk, enabling him to achieve self-control without losing self-esteem.

He begins to feed himself, dress himself and run around. If mother offers assistance in his trial-and-error experimenting, without humiliating him for incompetence, he develops confidence and is spared a feeling of overwhelming loneliness because he carries the memory of her presence. This is vital to his closeness/distance in future relationships, especially in marriage, where self-doubt and inadequacy can hinder his giving of himself to the symbiosis of intercourse and sharing of the secrets of his heart with his wife.

By the way, it is not without significance that, in Scandinavian countries, schooling does not start until the child is seven — when he loses his milk teeth he is also ready to be fully weaned from home as well.

b. Integration

Three basic urges characterise human beings — *self-preservation* (the desire to withdraw for security), plus two opposing desires that relate to reaching out for 'novelty', namely *aggression* and *love* (sex when practised in a godly attitude is a giving and receiving of love).

These correspond to the three sides of our parental triangle in lesson 1. The child *loves* because we first love him (compare 1 John 4:19, 'We love because [Jesus] first loved us'); our discipline provides secure boundaries, meeting his need for *self-preservation*; and within the scope of the freedom which we allow him he is able to vent his *aggression* into investigating and conquering the world.

Wholeness is the integrating of these diverging desires. Breast-feeding, for instance, is a very aggressive exercise which is also a means of enjoying mutual love. As we remarked in lesson 1, if aggression is allowed to get out of hand it produces a sense of guilt and self-criticism. But a mature person is well-integrated, with all his urges harnessed and harmonised. For example, a carpenter vents his *aggression* on wood, sawing, planing and hammering because he *loves* timber and shapes it creatively.

Let us review the child's development in its four dimensions and consider how we can contribute helpfully as parents.

1. Mental development

R.M. Restak informs us that one section of brain-cell growth in infants is stimulated by snuggling, rocking and cuddling — a parental ministry to his *urge for self-preservation and for love*.

In 1977 two American psychologists, Meltzoff and Moore, showed convincingly that newborn babies are not mindless, but capable of complex thought and clever skills, learning at an astonishing speed — faster than at any time in later life — and enjoying problem-solving, after which they quickly become bored.

A twelve-day-old baby, for example, would put out his tongue to imitate his mother. A forty-two-minute-old boy switched from tongue-poking to an open-mouthed 'Ah' shape when his mother changed her action. A five-month-old child can choose music from three ring-pulls and show a definite preference. Most of a group of fourteen-month-olds, shown a twenty-second demo video of how to dismantle and reassemble a plastic dumb-bell, could take one apart next day, in contrast to only ten per cent of a group who had only been shown a still picture of the toy.

The point for us as parents is to be aware that our babies are intelligent, and alert so that we do not limit our interaction with them to 'koochy-koo' conversations! We can play games that respect this intelligent ability of theirs to respond, varying our approach and so satisfying *the urge for aggressive investigation*.

And, since eighty per cent of a child's I.Q. is established in his first eight years, we can stimulate its growth by supplying creative materials — scissors, music, crayons, reading aloud, travel, teaching him to observe and describe what he sees, and answering his questions (if you don't know, you can always find out for him).

Check up on your children's school-work. Are they learning to think and understand or just to give 'right' answers? A good student really isn't bothered about pleasing adults so does not need effusive praise when he discovers the 'how' and the 'why' of things. The story *Mister God, this is Anna* (Fount) highlights this in a most illuminating way.

Bear in mind, too, that even when he gives a wrong answer, your child may have used some hidden logic that makes sense to *him!*

2. Physical development

Good food, right sleep patterns and exercise contribute to physical health. Exercise usually takes care of itself, if our four-year-old grandson is typical — he rarely walks anywhere, preferring to skip and hop!

On the media and in schools we are bombarded with sound advice on balanced nutrition and the avoidance of junk food, so there is little need to go into detail here. We recommend raising your children on a minimum of sugar products, limiting cakes and sweets to just before teeth-cleaning times. With hyperactive children, advice is freely available as to which chemical additives to avoid in preserved foods.

Children of all ages can frustrate themselves by attempting what they are not sufficiently developed to perform. Because the toddler's nerve-sheaths are not fully completed, his movements are big — from shoulders, waist and knees. Later he can manage wrist and ankle movements, such as writing and dribbling a football.

Junior can use tools and play musical instruments, but then, just when he seems neatly compact and well co-ordinated, he starts to fall over his fast-growing teenage feet during another gangly era of life! By age sixteen to eighteen he should be well-developed again.

3. Social development

In the course of his social progress the child passes through various phases. Awareness of these changes can spare us years of unnecessary worrying. The four- to seven-year-old, for instance, although still physically dependent on his parents, tends to have ideas of his own. In fact, he is fairly self-possessed and egocentric. Although grateful for his parents' care, he is not especially affectionate, and mother could be tempted to grieve that he is going to grow up to forget her and neglect her in her old age.

He now feels free to choose friends at school who have no association with his parents. But even with them he doesn't have a strong sense of social commitment. When he has finished his turn at batting he may sneak off home without fulfilling his fielding obligations while others bat.

Even in the seven-to-twelve age bracket the gang spirit is of a fairly *ad hoc* nature; they will meet up for some adventure and then disperse. (Read up on *Tom Sawyer* and *Just William* if you have a child in this age group!) He will accept authority — but preferably of his own choice (the scoutmaster or football coach).

Of the twelves to fourteens, boys are more gregarious than girls, who tend to be personal in their attachment (BF in the diary means Best Friend). Strong trends in clothes and activities (which can suddenly change) characterise this time of life.

Then your fifteen-year-old may be a loner, listening to his tapes and records. From sixteen years onwards the one-gender gang usually changes into a group of mixed membership, probably linked to some movement (social, political or religious), with national or international identity and ideals.

The child handles *possessions* in different social ways throughout his development. The two- to four-year-old probably has a special 'comforter'. Our grandson still returns to his much loved Teddy, a threadbare, one-eyed, half-nosed, restuffed, hole-poked 'bag of rags'. When he is established at school we anticipate his final weaning from this geriatric companion. When a toddler 'gives' one of his small 'treasures' to a friend to play with, he is beginning to venture into social development.

In the seven-to-twelve-year range, possessions become status symbols. Possessing a cricket bat can qualify him to organise a neighbourhood match. For twelves to fourteens, Dad's new car is a means of social boasting. And in the uncertain years of puberty, personal treasures can again become a means of comfort and of expressing friendship.

4. Spiritual development

We will go into this in more detail in lesson 6 — describing ways in which we can minister God's love to our children, inculcate faith in his Word, encourage thankfulness for his goodness, reverence for his sovereignty and obedience to his will.

2. Disruption

> *'The boy Samuel __________________ to _________ in ___________ and in ___________ with the Lord and with men.'*
>
> (1 Samuel 2:26)

This is not, unfortunately, the progress report on every child.

a. Symptoms of disruption

Instead of growing up to wholeness (the basic meaning of 'salvation' — 1 Peter 2:2), a child's development may become stunted in some areas, even into adult life. If his need of security, his sense of dependence, is not duly weaned from him and integrated, he can develop anxieties and fears. Or his phase of self-display can be perverted into exhibitionism, his curiosity into gossip and voyeurism.

As parents we do well to follow Solomon's advice to shepherds and elders:

> *'Be sure you ________ the __________________ of your flocks, ________ careful __________________ to your herds.'*
>
> (Proverbs 27:23)

A child who is gripped by an irrational fear may react in a physical way, experiencing headaches which cannot be accounted for, bed-wetting, a 'lump' in his throat or breathing difficulties. Or his behaviour may indicate his inner disturbance – rudeness, lying, daydreaming, withdrawing from other children or a dread of school each morning.

Children under ten years of age tend to express their real feelings in their paintings — but don't base your conclusion on a one-off picture, especially if only two crayons were available!

Child psychologists note:

1. The predominant colour

☐ green suggests self-reliance

☐ yellow that he is zealous but insecure

☐ blue implies growing self-control

☐ red, anger

☐ black or purple, despair

2. Details

☐ overpainting could indicate a psychological cover-up, e.g. red overpainted suggests *hidden* aggression

☐ the size of a character suggests its relative importance to the child

☐ missing arms or hands can be clues to envy; missing or distorted eyes, fingers, noses clues to anxiety

b. Causes of disruption

The cause may have arisen in any of the child's three main environments — the home, the school or the neighbourhood. For example, his teacher may discover that:

☐ he is abused or threatened at home

☐ his father is away on a business trip

Or his parents may become aware that:

☐ the child feels discouraged by a teacher

- ☐ he is being derided by a school friend
- ☐ a school friend has been seriously injured or killed
- ☐ he has heard some horror story from children in the street
- ☐ Great-Aunt Mavis screamed at the sight of ants when she took him on a picnic

The child is not always aware of what he actually fears. Among the most common childhood fears are:

- ☐ abandonment by parents
- ☐ guilt
- ☐ parental friction
- ☐ death
- ☐ failure

3. Deliverance

a. An event

In some instances a child will need the specific ministry of deliverance. This accords with the apostle Paul's statement to the Corinthians about *his* bringing *their* thoughts into obedience to Christ by means of his spiritual weapons of war. These weapons pulled down the Corinthians' uncontrollable reasonings and speculations, which were trying to undermine their experiential knowledge of God:

> *'They have divine power to demolish strongholds. We demolish arguments and every pretension that sets itself up against the knowledge of God, and we take captive ________ ________ to make it ________________ to Christ.'*
>
> (2 Corinthians 10:4-5)

Our older son, Ian, was taken to hospital at the age of three for a check-up after drinking and vomiting up a little paraffin. He resisted the five nurses and a doctor who tried to undress him and fled screaming along the corridor into his mother's arms. During the next two and half years he was very fearful of strangers and often had disturbed nights, until Hugh and David Mansell ministered deliverance to him. David saw in a vision a row of hospital beds, one overshadowed by a dark cloud, from which menacing hands stretched out. We spoke words of release in Jesus' name.

Soon afterwards, Ian invited Jesus into his life. His schoolteacher unwittingly testified to a radical change in his behaviour from that point in the school year, from fearful withdrawal to trusting co-operation. In adult life he enjoys people and will speak or sing before crowds unabashed.

b. Convalescence

Not all childhood disruptions require crisis ministry. A change in the way a child's parents treat him can have the desired therapeutic effect. The key is to know the truth:

> *'You will know the truth, and the __________ will set you free . . . . If the Son ________ you free, you will be ________ indeed.'*
>
> (John 8:32, 36)

'Truth' or 'reality' (as the Greek word *aletheia* may be translated) will enable us to recognise when any of those three basic urges have been perverted and how we can channel them again towards healthy development.

What, for instance, is the truth about an unduly dependent or fearful child whose *self-preservation* seems to work overtime? The truth will most likely reveal that he is being forced to do things that he is not yet ready to cope with. He needs a good dose of the reality of God's love through his father and mother.

> *'There is ____ ________ in love. But ____________ ________ drives out fear, because fear has to do with punishment [hath torment, KJV]. The one who fears is not made perfect in love.'*
>
> (1 John 4:18)

Unconditional love is just one side of the triangle of essential parental contributions to which we were introduced in lesson 1.

What aspect of truth can release an ill-tempered, overly aggressive child? His parents probably need to ease up on their repressive discipline. In the case of an excessively sensual child the opposite seems to be indicated — they have been indulging his every demand.

c. Some common problems

1. Regression

A young child may react in a jealous way to the arrival of a new baby. Although some are openly aggressive — biting, hitting, pinching — others regress into baby ways to secure mother's attention.

Don't call 'babyish' the things he wants to experience and 'grown up' the things he dreads. But encourage every *spontaneous* sign of maturing. Let him talk out his feelings. Avoid *excessive* attention to the baby in his presence. (Safeguard the baby, too.)

2. Aggressiveness

In the first two years, his rage is not against people — he tends to thump the floor! Like puppies and kittens, a child will not usually bite to hurt, unless he is conditioned to do so by humorous reactions from people.

In children over two, look for the cause. Bullying? Reading difficulties in early school years? Does he feel ridiculous, inadequate, resentful?

3. Lying

Is it just *fantasy* appropriate to his very young age, when reality and make-believe are intertwined?

Is it because of *fear* — in self-defence because he can't *tell* you he hates his baby brother?

Does he need deliverance because it is chronic?

If you are in doubt, don't commit yourself into accusing him; respond to his lie with a casual, 'You don't say!'

Use trap questions to prevent lying. Not '*Did* you break the Dresden china lady?' but '*How* did you . . . ?'

4. Stealing

Was it just 'borrowing' in some vague optimistic hope of repaying later? Or is it deeper, to buy favours? Attention? To get even?

5. Laziness/dawdling

Is he tired? Ill? Worried (because misunderstood or belittled/ bored)?

The latter may be the case with an eight-year-old developing independence from a very efficient mother. Don't nag, but turn over a new leaf. Explain that you want him/her out from under your shadow and carrying more responsibility for his life. Let the other parent monitor the new arrangements: he will be called just once, breakfast will be ready — it's up to him after that. Maybe on the *first* morning, drive him to school if he is going to be late.

Don't get caught in a bribe/blackmail syndrome. 'You'll get no sweets if you're late' is a reminder of the old nag-prod routine!

6. Obesity

If this is due to 'comfort-eating' then the cause is emotional — probably insecurity. Don't deride!

Use the 'no-lose' contract: 'If you'll forego *this*, I'll give up *that*.' Especially watch *soft drinks*.

7. School phobia

It is better to make the child go to school, even if at first he sits in the head teacher's office — at least he has got over the dread of leaving the house.

8. Failure

Provide an area in which the child *can* succeed. Remember the tree in the school's backyard (lesson 2)? When a seven-year-old remedial maths boy climbed unaided to the first branch, his maths improved from that day on — he realised that he could succeed in one area, so maybe he could make it in the other.

9. The Oedipus complex

This causes a young boy to want to marry his mum, or a young girl her dad. This can lead to guilt and jealousy. Be aware of this without being worried, and don't ridicule. Some girls feel they have been deprived of a penis, or boys may fear to lose theirs (especially if someone jokes about the ducks pecking it off if he doesn't do up his trouser zip!). If you sense that these are worries he *isn't* voicing you can raise the question: 'Is a cow a mummy or a daddy?' as a conversation starter.

10. Bed-wetting

Ascertain that it isn't one of the rare cases with a physical cause (too small a bladder, etc.). Often it is the son of an over-efficient mother who fusses. He dreams of powerful persons, animals or forces (wind, sea, etc.) and wets like an excited puppy. He *feels incompetent*. It is no use holding him over the lavatory half-asleep: that only teaches him to urinate *in* his sleep! The best approach is to 'turn over a new leaf' of parental leniency.

****

LESSON 4

Deliverance and Development

True or False

1. T F Weaning is a feature of personal development.

2. T F Integration of all natural urges is essential to the achieving of maturity.

3. T F Among normal, basic human urges are pacifism and the death wish.

4. T F A newborn babe is a mindless creature incapable of problem-solving.

5. T F A two-year-old needs to be set a daily regime of physical exercises to prevent the stunting of his growth.

6. T F Alert parents will easily recognise when one of their children is disturbed.

7. T F Fear of abandonment is common in early childhood.

8. T F God has given us spiritual weapons with which to deliver our disturbed children.

9. T F The Greek word *aletheia* means 'sincerity'.

10. T F There is only ever *one* reason why a child tells a lie.

Group Discussion

1. Compare notes on how some young children are natural mental investigators while others are physical explorers.

2. Make your observations on the various stages of a child's social development as outlined in section 1b(3.) of this lesson.

3. Share helpful testimonies on deliverance from any of the disruptions mentioned in the lesson notes.

Personal Assignments

'Be *sure* you know the condition of your flocks.'

1. Check out those areas of your parenting about which God convicted you as you studied this lesson.

2. Not all disturbances are obvious:

   - ☐ Do you *expect* your first-born to do all 'the dirty jobs' because she always volunteers? Does she volunteer because she thinks you expect her to?

   - ☐ Is the 'family baby' still indulged by you all, at *his* age?

   - ☐ Do any of your children have hidden fears? Ask God for the wisdom to find out and redress them.

True or False

1.T 2.T 3.F 4.F 5.F 6.T 7.T 8.T 9.F 10.F

LESSON 5

All-round Discipline

No, discipline is not just a clip round the ear and a good telling off. Discipline means training, and punishment is only one facet of it. Your neighbour may liberally deal out punishment to your child (e.g. shouting at him for walking over his prize chrysanthemums), but is unlikely to take an on-going interest in your child's development.

We cannot hope to improve on God's methods of discipline. They come to us in three categories:

Preventive — by his protection ('You hem me in — behind and before; you have laid your hand upon me' — Psalm 139:5), and his forewarnings (as when Jesus told self-confident Peter that he would deny him)

Corrective — by his crucible of hardships, which removes the dross of sin (1 Peter 1:7), his rod of painful consequences, which removes folly (Hebrews 12:5-11), and his pruning-knife of restrictions, which removes the 'good' wood which is the enemy of 'the best' (John 15:2), namely, bigger fruit

Directive — by his Word (which is for 'training in righteousness' – 2 Timothy 3:16-17) and his yoke (Matthew 11:29-30)

The end-product of God's disciplining of us, and of our disciplining of our children, is *self*-discipline in all three categories:

Preventive — such as shutting out distractions (Matthew 6:6), developing a routine and making oneself accountable to someone

Corrective — such as asking forgiveness when we realise we have been wrong, and denying ourselves pleasure in order to make time to catch up on a backlog of duties or to save money to keep out of debt

Directive — such as planning time for planning, and setting long-term goals and interim stages for achieving them

We must approach our task of disciplining thoughtfully so that we do not frustrate our children by harsh punishment or inconsistency:

> *'Fathers, do not ____________ your children, or they will become ____________________.'*
>
> (Colossians 3:21)

or prevent them, by bad example, from experiencing the Lord for themselves:

> *'______ the little children ________ ____ ____, and do not hinder them.'*
>
> (Mark 10:14)

Rather, we aim to train them to obey us because it is right, and to honour us and other authority figures because it is a means of blessing:

> *'Children, ________ your parents in the Lord, for this is ___________. "_____________ your father and mother . . . that it may ____ ______ with you." '*
>
> (Ephesians 6:1-3)

1. Preventive Discipline

a. A consistent example

If father is regularly inconsiderate and insensitive to his children, what hope has he of teaching *them* to be thoughtful? However, let every father take heart: even an imperfect example is better than none at all.

The cute little girl whose father died before she was born charmed every man she met. But in adult life she brought out chivalry in many an eligible bachelor, only to walk out on him as soon as she discovered he was not flawless. She had grown up with a fantasy image of the male of the species, never having had a real-life model in a father, big brother, uncle or close male family friend who could say no, be forgetful and show occasional fear or anger.

b. Clear rules

Rules need to be reduced to a minimum and be jointly agreed by father and mother, and understood by grandparents, childminders and older brothers and sisters so that they can be adhered to consistently.

Remember, your child will *have* to encounter authority sooner or later in life. It not only prevents anarchy but is the essence of the kingdom — the rule or government of God.

For you to be a true authority to your child he has to become aware that you know more about a subject than he does and that you can, and will, enforce what you ask without vacillating. So, establish early in his life that your word can be relied on, so that later on he can find support and direction from you.

For instance, you *can* tie him in a high-chair and hold him from wriggling while you dress him — these are physically provable facts. But you *cannot* follow through such common commands as: 'Eat your food up! Fill that potty — not your pants! Go to sleep! Stop crying this minute!'

Again, it is pointless wasting time trying to train him into ways he will grow into anyway — potty training, weaning, walking, feeding and dressing himself. Wayne Dennis once conducted a somewhat cruel experiment on twin girls who were semi-deprived for their first nine months. Despite that, they developed all their physical abilities normally. Even a deaf child will babble and a blind child will smile.

We now list a few practical rules appropriate for each stage of the child's development that will maintain a wise balance between routine and freedom (remember our triangle in lesson 1?). His freedom should not be at the expense of others' property or feelings — this prepares him for a responsible place in society.

A young child cannot grasp abstract ideas or complicated instruction. You will need to crouch down to his level to tell him the rule, and to get feedback from him that shows he actually understands.

1. 0-4 months

He should be free to ask for food when he feels hungry and to refuse when he feels full.

2. 4-6 months

He should be trained into a routine. Let him cry as he awaits feed-time. Walk him about if you will, but teach him that a slight discomfort does not merit full-scale attention.

3. 6-12 months

He can sit up, crawl, stand, handle objects and resist dressing, leave his high-chair and feed himself. Mother needs to realise that she does not have to keep up incessant conversation, and that she can go into another room without him. She should keep most of her playtime till near the end of his wakeful periods.

4. 1-2 years

He can walk and probably climb and needs freedom to experiment (are your stairs safe?). Watch out for hot liquids, peanuts, metal edges, poisons, etc.

Think ahead as to how you will handle bedtime frolics when he graduates from his cot to 'a big bed'! He will soon learn how to slip downstairs and appear suddenly looking adorably cute. Promise yourself in advance that you will not succumb.

Don't lock his bedroom door, but how about a low gate across the door? And when he grizzles or hollers what do you plan to do? It may sharpen your wits if you *imagine* that staying in his bed is vital for his health, or what you would do if he shouted down for the twentieth time! (We are assuming, of course, that you will not play boisterous games with him just before bedtime causing increased adrenaline, but will give him a warm bath followed by a story in his bed, and that you will leave a dim light on.)

5. 2-5 years

You will need to establish some do's and don'ts about eating practices:

- ☐ he is only allowed to eat between meals if he eats enough at mealtimes
- ☐ he should only eat meals at the table
- ☐ once he has left the table and it has been cleared, that's it till the next spread ('the dawdler's rule'!)

Let's not over-fuss the child in this age bracket who tends to peck at his food like a sparrow, maybe after an illness. The normal rate of weight increase drops considerably in these years. And why *must* he eat his vegetables? We used to know a fine specimen of athletic manhood who had avoided them entirely throughout his childhood — he got his vital vitamins and fibre from fruit.

6. Early school days, 6-7 years

Now is the time for teaching them to cross the road alone and for training on two-wheeled bicycles.

7. School years

Tidiness is virtually unknown among healthy school-kids. *Must* his bedroom be spick and span? Do mealtimes require Buckingham Palace etiquette? Common decency is the maximum requirement. For example, don't put genteel Aunt Agatha off her cucumber sandwiches by an open-mouthed display of half-digested morsels.

Because the gang's influence is paramount, now is the time for clear parental advice on the right peer group from which to choose personal friends.

8. Teens

More on this time of life in lesson 7. Just to say for now: treat your teens as you would the sons or daughters of very good friends — listen a lot and advise only sparingly and on vital issues unless your views have been sought.

c. Organising and overseeing

A very young convalescing child finds it hard to stay in bed doing nothing. Swap him from bed to bed at intervals. Give him a bell to ring for service.

The child reported by his teacher to be well behaved at school usually becomes over-active when he gets home. Help him run off his pent-up energy.

In the teenage years when they have to cope with invitations to wild parties and unhealthy discos don't be afraid to put *your* foot down firmly but politely. Assure them they can blame the refusal completely on you when explaining it to their friends. Often they will thank you that you gave them an early deadline for returning home because they could see the party was getting out of hand.

How should we deal with their quarrels among themselves? Watch for the underlying reasons. Is it *retaliation* — taking it out on the other because he is often picked on by you? Is it *jealousy* because you frequently compare him with the others? Don't get trapped in the fair-play syndrome, because real life is very unequal! And don't be too keen to offer your services as arbiter: that role is best taken when *both* sides want a 'court settlement'.

d. Not yielding to his whims

1. Whining

If the young child is a habitual whiner, become aware of the pattern. When does he whine? (Is he a rainy-day whiner?) To whom? (Does he ever do it to Dad?) Why? (Is he missing a friend who has moved or just started school?)

Notice if you have been reinforcing his habit: Have your ears been 'switching off' his babble *until* he whines — so he knows that's how to speak to get your attention? Tell him that mummies have strange ears that pick up messages best when he asks in a normal voice politely.

2. Tantrums

If he is four and has never had a tantrum, you have probably never taught him the realities of life — that there are limits. If he is two and has one a month — or one a day — he is learning about life and has the gumption to resent it once in a while. But if he scores three or four per day examine your style:

☐ Are you making too many demands on him?

☐ Do you try to teach him too much at one time?

☐ Does he feel unsure who loves him?

To teach him that a tantrum is not an effective device, walk out of the room or deposit him in another part of the house which is safe and toy-free — it is hard to create a fuss without an audience.

☐ Don't try to outroar him or ridicule him

☐ Don't try to explain rules to him at this point

☐ Don't offer him a bribe — he can 'up' his price!

Watch out for variation on the theme:

☐ spitting (*never* think it cute)

☐ biting and kicking (restrain him)

☐ vomiting (put him in his cot while you mop up and go on to do something interesting to distract him)

☐ breath-holding (don't worry, at the worst he could faint, but he will not die!)

As he learns to verbalise his feelings he will have no need for histrionics.

e. Not reacting impulsively

The teacher who used to shout her protests with increasing decibels until she leapt on a desk and blew a whistle got 'wound up' deliberately by her class, who enjoyed the purposeless show.

2. Corrective Discipline

In any situation where a child has overstepped the line, ascertain what actually happened. Take age and motive into account when it is a matter of accident or damage that did not involve any breach of rules.

Seven-year-old Anthony felt like leaving home when told off for removing slates from the roof to let daylight in on his dark attic den — he expected to be enthusiastically congratulated for his ingenuity! And, as one mother agreed as she surveyed the soggy carpet, 'There was no rule: thou shall not carry tomato soup from kitchen to dining-room on roller skates!'

Young children can be sensitive to parents' emotions. Explosive anger can damage them; they can cope with verbalised anger, but are affected if they see we are grieved by their behaviour. One lad said as he sat quietly sobbing on the stairs, 'I don't mind the *angry* bit, but I don't like the *sad* bit!'

a. Natural consequences

'You've hurt yourself. If you had done what I said this would never have happened.'

b. Deprive of special privileges

But be sure the child *feels* deprived. For instance, withhold cakes from Master Sweet Tooth, clothes from Miss Show-off, money from the Big Spender and a favourite TV programme from young Square Eyes.

c. Restitution when necessary

For example, take him to hand back a stolen toy or party cakes; make her do an hour's gardening for arriving home an hour late.

d. The rod for rebellion

The object is *not* to beat rebellion out of him but to settle up for the act of disobedience (see Proverbs 22:15; 13:24; 29:15; Hebrews 12:5-6, 13, 15).

1. Act immediately

Don't say, 'Wait till your dad gets home.'

2. Take him aside

Remove him from the gloating eyes of his siblings. This also helps you to cool down.

3. See that he understands his 'crime'

4. Make the smack an event, not an impulse

The family 'comedian' may try to make you laugh to put you off your stroke. The correct response is: 'I may be laughing but I'll still have to smack you, son.'

Scripture mentions the rod — a neutral object.

'The hand should only be used for blessing,' reckons one school of thought. 'Your hand will hurt if you inflict too much pain,' says the other.

Many a child would choose a smack rather than giving up something.

5. Allow him to cry — in peace

6. The parent who punished should be the first to cuddle him

e. Take him to the church elders

This is, of course, a last resort (see Matthew 18:15-17).

3. Directive Discipline

a. Example

Desirable character traits cannot be instilled by lecturing, arguments, nagging or pep-talks. In fact, such efforts can warp the child's personality. Rather, children imbibe the standards they have *seen* in their parents.

1. Bravery (in a preschool child)

'He runs away from smaller boys,' bleats Mother. Well, he can only learn one lesson at a time, either:

- ☐ to kick, bite, scratch, shove; or
- ☐ that none of those are socially acceptable (e.g. jumping on Suzy's tummy), so he has recourse to the wisdom of the courts (he runs and tells his parents), a principle still true in his adult life

Bravery is a complex virtue. Your child needs also to know that if he gets defeated in a fight, he is still loved. Even Lord Mountbatten was frequently bullied at school.

By about ten years or older he can *begin* to learn: 'That punch he landed on your nose won't hurt for long. Not retaliating was a very brave decision.'

2. Sportsmanship

What *is* sportsmanship? Enjoying being defeated? Lying with a forced smile? Taking unfair advantage of a handicapped opponent?

Again, the child will learn by example — how *you* keep the younger 'brats' at bay when he is not allowed to hit back. And how you handle your car relative to slow pedestrians and dilatory drivers.

3. Generosity ('sharing')

A young child is honest and direct. He sees what he wants, takes it and keeps it.

At two to three years he will share if he gets something better in return (it's called 'horse-trading' in the Wild West).

At five to six years he will share if a scowling adult is present; or willingly give in return for praise (more horse trading!).

At ten to twelve he will share cheerfully (if approval is given).

At sixteen he will share and give himself a pat on the back. At this *and* earlier ages he can give as 'to the Lord': here we go beyond secular sense.

4. Self-confidence

You may be tempted to worry about an over-confident preschooler. He is likely to get it knocked out of him by his peers in the course of life.

If he is afraid of failure, provide a context in which he can succeed: achieving in music, sports, etc.

5. Responsibility (self-control; industriousness)

Assigning chores will not guarantee he will learn to be responsible. They can lead to friction. They can teach him: When I'm big enough I'll off-load undesirable tasks.

Rather, show him by gratuitously helping him yourself. As he gets into his teens *thrust* some decision on him.

b. Instruction

Knowledge not only prevents unnecessary fears but can positively stimulate growth in confidence. Rosemary took time to teach our sons — as well as our daughters — to cook. Only Hugh is still desperately ignorant in domestic techniques!

If we don't take the initiative in the sex education of our own children they are liable to be taught from a humanistic viewpoint at school without the moral safeguards of God's Word. We recommend *Help! I'm Growing Up — A child/parent guide to sex and puberty* by Roger and Christine Day (Harvestime) as a textbook to read with them and discuss together.

c. Assist

Offering to help them in certain tasks will communicate motivation to a degree that the mere issuing of executive commands never will. You may actually *enjoy* cleaning out the garage with him, and he with you.

d. Rewards

Wall-charts, with stars for achievement, can be useful as memory joggers if played as a game. James Dobson suggests giving to children as long-term prizes, after they have collected a certain number of stars, items you would *have* to buy anyway (football boots, etc.). The short-term rewards would be your praise and the coloured stars on the chart. But whether the system produces real character change is very doubtful: when the 'bribes' stop there is likely to be a lapse in behaviour patterns.

But they can be fun for Mum to use when Dad is away on a business trip, such as to encourage teeth cleaning or music practice.

- ☐ Be sure to set attainable goals
- ☐ Reinforce what is *near* to your ideal in his present behaviour

e. No-lose contracts

No-lose contracts include agreeing that if the child will do 'A', you will do 'B'. 'I want you to wear your school cap in this damp weather; I will take my umbrella.'

LESSON 5

All-round Discipline

True or False

1. T F To discipline means to punish.
2. T F God's discipline includes preventive measures and directives as well as correction.
3. T F The child's self-discipline is the ultimate aim of parental discipline.
4. T F We can hinder and embitter our children by harsh discipline.
5. T F Consistent example and clear rules make for good discipline.
6. T F Perfect potty-training is a vital foundation to consistent adult behaviour.
7. T F Discipline should start when the child first attends school.
8. T F The rod is the only means of discipline taught in Scripture.
9. T F Good character traits are best inculcated by parental example.
10. T F Behaviour charts and rewards are the only effective means of establishing long-term good habits of behaviour.

Group Discussion

1. Talk over the fact that all-round discipline involves prevention and direction as well as correction. Illustrate this from God's ways of disciplining us.
2. Discuss which aspect of corrective discipline is most appropriate to different kinds of offences: natural consequences, depriving of special privileges, the rod, etc.

3. Share together your observations about character development in a child at various stages of his life in such matters as bravery, self-confidence, responsibility, etc.

Personal Assignment

1. Design a behaviour and duties chart (e.g. remembering to clean teeth at bedtime, putting pyjamas away before school, piano practice). Decide on rewards.

2. Discuss as a couple:

   - ☐ Have you set too many rules?
   - ☐ Are the rules clear to each child?
   - ☐ Are you consistent in applying them?
   - ☐ Are you agreed on them as a couple?
   - ☐ Do you oversee and organise your family enough? Too much?

True or False

1.F 2.T 3.T 4.T 5.T 6.F 7.F 8.F 9.T 10.F

LESSON 6

Playing and Praying

1. Recognise Your Children's Heritage

a. The kingdom belongs to them

'Little children were brought to Jesus for him to place his hands on them and pray for them. But the disciples rebuked those who brought them. Jesus said, "Let the ________ ________ ________ to me, and do not hinder them, for the ________ ____ ________ ________ to ________ ____ ________."'

(Matthew 19:13-14)

The parents who brought these infants were not only Israelites but 'Israelites indeed' who were not antagonistic to the Messianic words and works of Jesus. The apostle Paul assures us that even children with just one believing parent have a head start on the road to the kingdom. He was referring to a pagan marriage in which one spouse becomes a Christian:

'If any brother has a wife who is not a believer and she is willing to live with him, he must not divorce her. And if a woman has a husband who is not a believer and he is willing to live with her, she must not divorce him. For the unbelieving husband has been ________ through his wife, and the unbelieving wife has been sanctified through her believing husband. Otherwise your ________ would be unclean, but as it is, they are ________.'

(1 Corinthians 7:12-14)

Our children are set apart (sanctified) from the defiling and distracting influences of unclean spirits. This does not mean that salvation is automatic. A rich spiritual heritage 'belongs' to the Jews (Romans 9:4-5 NASB) but even their religious leaders like Nicodemus 'must be born again' (John 3:3, 5). In the same way, a Christian's children and unbelieving spouse still need to enter the kingdom to be 'saved' (see v16).

Note, incidentally, that not one drop of baptismal water is sprinkled anywhere in 1 Corinthians 7; what safeguards our children's spiritual welfare is not christening but *our* godliness.

b. Their angels appear before God

> *'See that you do not look down on one of these ____________ ________ . For I tell you that __________ ____________ in heaven always ______ the face of my ____________ in heaven.'*
>
> (Matthew 18:10)

That is the case even though, as the Master went on to explain, they are lost sheep (v12-14). Therefore we ought to present them to the Lord from before their birth — John the Baptist was filled with the Spirit while in Elizabeth's womb (Luke 1:15 margin; 1:44) — and treat them like Cornelius: included though not yet reborn (see Acts 10, especially v1-6; also 11:13-14). Their inclusion is not because they were born in innocence, but because of the atoning value of Jesus' shed blood.

We learned the reality of these promises very early in our calling to parenthood. When our eldest child, Grace, was only three years and nine months she announced at breakfast one morning that she had asked Jesus into her heart — 'And I asked him in to stay.'

No appeal had been made at the children's meeting the night before nor had there been any reference to receiving Christ, yet she had spontaneously opened her life to the Lord. Although we were tempted to 'wait and see', Grace repeatedly claimed that event as her moment of decision. She was baptised in water and in the Spirit at the age of nine, and joined her husband in full-time pastoral ministry at twenty-three.

2. Help Them Attain Their Birthright

Some parents kneel by the empty grate of their child's heart and cry to God to light a miraculous fire. Others rake out the ashes of sin, lay the sticks, coal and firelighters of godliness, wisdom and truth, then pray for the Lord to send a spark! They also regulate the draught of faith, apply the poker of discipline and add more fuel of biblical revelation in order to increase the heat.

What are the best methods to produce spirituality in our children? A colleague, while on his travels, conducted a private survey of parents who had succeeded in bringing up their children as balanced individuals, children who now walked with God consistently and fruitfully in their own right. What ingredients did they have in common in their programme of spiritual training?

Amazingly, they all had this one identical practice: none of them had a regimented schedule of devotional exercises, a regular 'family altar'!

Our family is no exception. From time to time, according to the ages and interests of the children, we conducted seasons of devotional exercises, but not every day of the week even then. We found most 'family-altar helps' were either theoretical or sentimentally unreal. Dead works carried out legalistically only stifle faith and choke life. It is:

> *'the ________ of God that . . . . teaches us to say "No" to ungodliness and worldly passions, and to live self-controlled, upright and godly lives',*
>
> (Titus 2:11)

and:

> *'God's ______________ leads you towards repentance.'*
>
> (Romans 2:4)

If a practice has borne fruit for you, don't ruin things by turning it into a law; and when a principle works, don't fossilise it as a formula!

We here offer guidelines that have worked successfully for us.

a. Worship in reality

The kind of worshippers the Father seeks are the genuine sort who worship him in sincerity and reality (see John 4:23; Greek *aletheia*, truth or reality).

Singing a few Scripture songs out of routine duty, even if with great gusto, will not lead our children to an enjoyment of God.

It must appear unreal to a child to hear her father say, 'I love you, Lord,' when she has never known him remark, 'I love you, sweetheart,' to her mother!

To help prime the pump:

- ☐ Express your appreciation of one another
- ☐ Count your blessings. (What has made you happy today?)
- ☐ Consider God's handiwork (even the very young can grasp God's wonders in creation, e.g. Psalm 8; 29; 98:1-7); make a collage of seeds and leaves
- ☐ Sing Scripture (toddlers will join in with delight, uttering words whose meaning is beyond them)
- ☐ Write a letter to Jesus
- ☐ Express self-acceptance: 'Thank you, God, for making me me'; 'Susies are good for you . . . our family needs this Susie, she is . . . '; 'My friends like me because . . .'
- ☐ Rejoice in tribulation — Corrie and Betsie ten Boom in Ravensbruck concentration camp thanked God for:

– each other's company

– the smuggled Bible

– a captive audience to whom to read it, and

– the fleas that kept the guards away!

What is 'bugging' us right now? What 'fleas' can we thank God for today?

1. Children's worship is acceptable to God

> *'When the chief priests and the teachers of the law saw the wonderful things he did and the children shouting in the temple area, "Hosanna to the Son of David," they were indignant. "Do you hear what these children are saying?" they asked him. "Yes,"*

> *replied Jesus, "have you never read, 'From the _________ ____ _____________ and infants you have ordained_____________?" '*
>
> (Matthew 21:15-16)

Although those children were merely repeating what they had heard the crowd singing earlier (v9) — snatches of a seasonal carol, part of the Great Hallel liturgy (Psalms 113 — 118) sung at Passover time (Psalm 118:27) — they were in spiritual harmony with the choirs of heaven, who also sing, 'Salvation . . . to our God' (Revelation 19:1). 'Hosanna' means 'Save now'.

2. Youthful praise silences demons

The lad David's ministry to the Lord on his harp in the presence of demonised King Saul demonstrates this.

b. Pray in faith

Our prayers should be in faith — not in unconvinced fatalism ('if it be thy will') nor in mere optimism.

☐ *Focus on specifics*, e.g. problems at school

☐ *Be conversational*. Pray with your child, not at him

☐ *Ask within the limits of true faith*. You may not be in faith for the man next door to be converted, but you may have faith to make contact during this week, or that he will come for coffee and raise a problem about which you can pray with him

☐ *Keep a record* of the more significant requests and the testimonies of the answers

c. Teach heart-to-heart

– not just mentally and factually.

1. Instil the commandments of God

Let us remind ourselves of God's directions to parents through Moses on how to impart his commandments:

> *'Hear, O Israel: The Lord our God, the Lord is one. Love the Lord your God with all your heart and with all your soul and with all your strength. These commandments that I give you today are to be upon your hearts. Impress them on your children. Talk about them when you sit at home and when you walk along the road, when you lie down and when you get up. Tie them as symbols on your hands and bind them on your foreheads. Write them on the door-frames of your houses and on your gates.'*
>
> (Deuteronomy 6:4-9)

Note carefully the sequence of instructions:

i. Know, love and obey God yourself. Let your family see how you submit to God's Word gladly when you are tempted to cheat and compromise in order to maintain popularity or gain promotion.

ii. Impress his commands on your children, like a signet ring on hot wax.

iii. Talk about them situationally, relating God's ways to everyday life.

iv. Fix them indelibly in your activities ('hands') and thinking ('foreheads').

v. Then apply them as you and your household move out into the world ('door-frames') and into the church ('gates' — where the elders hold council). Respecting parents at home trains your children to respect God's delegated authority in school, at work, in the nation and in the church.

2. Recount God's ways

Tell of God's ways from the Bible, history and your own testimony:

> *'What our fathers have told us . . . . We will not hide them from their children; we will tell the next generation the praiseworthy deeds of the Lord . . . so that the next generation . . . in turn would tell their children. Then they would put their trust in God and would not forget his deeds but would keep his commands. They would not be like their forefathers — a stubborn and rebellious generation, whose hearts were not loyal to God, whose spirits were not faithful to him.'*
>
> (Psalm 78:3-8)

Our frequent, enthusiastic reiterating of God's faithful dealings with his covenant people — how he faithfully disciplined them for their sins and faithfully blessed them for their obedience — will establish our youngsters as a stable people amid an inconsistent generation.

3. Instruct them creatively

Bear in mind the age, temperament and spiritual state of each child. Use his natural bent: Is he a good reader? Then let him read the verses aloud.

Arouse curiosity: you can lead a horse to water and he is sure to drink if you first put salt in his oats! For instance, let the child pretend to be part of the crowd, or even a leading character in the story. How did he feel as he lived it out? Tell him what to look for before you read the passage: Who in the incident is angry? Puzzled? Troubled? Calm? Excited? Can he spot the mystery word or deliberate mistake? (Choose a *significant* word or mistake.)

d. Discuss with purpose

Raise discussion on vital issues in the news, in the day's experience or in some TV drama.

1. Use questions not of mere fact but of intent:

☐ What do you think is the purpose of . . . ?

☐ How do you think this applies to us?

2. Prompt their questions (Exodus 13:14-16; Deuteronomy 6:20-25)

3. Train them to decide courageously like Daniel (Daniel 6) and his friends (Daniel 3), and all the heroes and heroines of faith in Hebrews 11. A dead fish floats downstream; a living salmon can leap up waterfalls and swim against the current. Rejoice with them that we are the truly normal people on this planet!

4. Be aware of each child's concept of goodness and truth. The toddler, you will observe, tends to live in a world of make-believe, so he believes what he *says*. Probably few preadolescent children actually hate lying; they tell the truth mainly to avoid adult disapproval. However, stealing is a crime in their reckoning because it threatens their own property. Teenagers feel angry at social injustice, talk about putting the world right and want short-cuts to perfection!

e. Play with enjoyment

Whatever you choose to play, let it be for *mutual* enjoyment. Hugh likes to read aloud using different accents for the various characters, and the children enjoyed being read to even when they were well able to read for themselves. However, Rosemary can't stand being read to or reading aloud; instead she liked to cook with the family — even the boys found it fun.

To a child, play is a 'means of grace' (see Zechariah 8:5; Matthew 11:16-17). While at play they can learn a lot of basic spiritual lessons. Time must be booked in advance for this to be effective.

Here are some suggestions:

1. Read a story together — but switch off the TV first.

2. Watch TV together.

3. Arrange a communal cook-up: one collects the ingredients, another measures them, someone else mixes them together.

4. Games instil various lessons. *Uno* reminds us of the uncertainties and surprises of life. *Boggle* helps with simple spelling. *Nature Trail* imparts facts of God's creation. *Jigsaws* give opportunity for team co-operation. *Chequers and chess* emphasise that you have to think ahead in life to win.

5. Nostalgia night with the family photo-album, when holiday memories can be revived and stories of great-great-grandma recollected.

6. Make a banner or mural.

7. Visit a park, museum, library; buy an ice-cream in town instead of digging one out of the freezer at home.

LESSON 6

Playing and Praying

True or False

1. T F The kingdom of God is the birthright of our children.
2. T F Christening our babies is their guarantee of godliness in later life.
3. T F A child of three years cannot be aware of Jesus.
4. T F Family devotions must be 'in life' to be fruitful.
5. T F To worship God in reality, it helps to begin by thanking him for his handiwork and the blessings he has bestowed on us.
6. T F Children's singing of Scripture is offensive to God's ear unless they fully understand what the words mean.
7. T F We should regularly impart to our children a knowledge of God's commandments and his great works in times past.
8. T F Questions and answers help children to learn.
9. T F Playing with children hinders them from knowing the Lord.

Group Discussion

1. Tell each other of examples of young children's experiences of God.
2. Talk together about methods of 'family devotions' you have known that were productive, and some that were barren.
3. Share ideas for family fun times.
4. Advise one another on how to adapt teaching and activities to various ages and temperaments.

Personal Assignment

1. Book a regular night for family fun. Plan activities that will be mutually enjoyable. (Ask each one for suggestions.)

2. Map out a four-week programme for family worship:

   - ☐ Bible readings
   - ☐ Memory verses
   - ☐ Questions
   - ☐ Stories
   - ☐ Activities

   Stay in reality:

   - ☐ What time can you reasonably give?
   - ☐ What concentration are they capable of?

3. Assess as parents how you can improve your presentation to the children, e.g. more excitement when you testify to answered prayer — saving up the news in order to make an event of telling it at the meal table.

True or False

1.T 2.F 3.F 4.T 5.T 6.F 7.T 8.T 9.F

LESSON 7

Transition Through Teens

So, you've got teenagers in your family now. Or perhaps that time is still some way off. Does the prospect of those teen years seem daunting? Don't panic or despair — you will succeed as parents.

After all, *you* apparently survived this chrysalis stage between childhood and adult maturity. And that was probably before 'teenage' had been invented! As the old King James Bible often says: 'and it came *to pass'!*

If you laid a good foundation in earlier years your teenagers will still be your friends. But you now need to understand them all over again.

And, even if you have only recently put your life under the lordship of Christ, his promise to you is:

> *'I will __________ you for the years the locusts have eaten,'*
>
> (Joel 2:25)

twice adding the assurance:

> *'Never again will my people be ____________ .'*
>
> (Joel 2:26, 27)

If you have returned to the Lord as he requires (Joel 2:13) and placed yourselves under his outpoured Spirit then –

> *'Your ________ and ___________________ will ______________ ,'*
>
> (Joel 2:28)

even in their turbulent days of adolescence.

1. Pressure Areas

Let's remind ourselves of Dr Luke's diagnosis of Jesus' healthy development during his teenage years:

> *'Jesus grew in ____________ [mentally] and ____________ [physically], and in ____________ with God [spiritually] and men [socially].'*
>
> (Luke 2:52)

a. Physical pressures

1. Bodily changes

The adolescent has new bodily functions to cope with: your daughter needs to understand about premenstrual tension, and your son about nocturnal emissions ('wet dreams'). 'Boy meets girl' attraction can be as intense as Romeo and Juliet — they 'fall in love' at first sight, only to 'fall out of love' just as swiftly.

2. Embarrassment

They may experience new embarrassment — delayed development of sexual organs compared with most in their school class; the unreliability of the boy's breaking voice; sudden spurts of growth that cause your daughter to stoop or your son to trip over his canal-barge feet.

3. Emotions

They will encounter mood swings due to hormonal changes. Boredom is the third major cause of teenage suicide in Britain. They may withdraw, daydream or achieve lower grades at school due to a shortened attention span. Depression can hit them. Some may attempt to express their depression in promiscuity, drugs or theft. The teenager at times feels bewildered.

'Why are you crying, love?' Hugh asked one of our daughters when she was in her mid-teens.

'I don't know, Daddy,' she admitted.

He assured her she was simply growing up and it was OK to cry!

b. Mental pressures

1. Questioning

He will query beliefs he once held clearly. He has to find out for himself. Even the twelve-year-old Jesus implied that this urge is normal when he asked Joseph and Mary why they had been anxiously searching for him.

> *'Didn't you know I ______ ____ ____ in my Father's house?'*
>
> (Luke 2:49)

He had spent a couple of days

> *'in the temple courts, sitting among the teachers, ______________________ to them and ______________ them __________________ .'*
>
> (Luke 2:46)

2. Uncertainties

Her dogmatic opinions only cover up her uncertainties. Don't be alarmed. Settled convictions take time to form; they are the fruit of much experience.

3. Rationally irrational

He believes he is being rational when he tries to justify some theory with a handful of disjointed ideas.

4. Idealism and hero-worship can feature prominently during this phase of development. They are ready to sign up for the latest revolution!

5. Protest music

Many teenagers prefer their music loud, with a beat and some message of protest.

6. Self-consciousness suddenly increases. When they were younger the important thing was prowess ('What I can do'); now the all-absorbing concern can be: 'Who am I?' and: 'How do I look?' We must handle their self-esteem with care.

c. Social pressures

1. Conformity and fashion loom large. What will their set/gang think? They may not want to bring their friends home in case they should disapprove of our 'old-fashioned' ways.

2. Career prospects are often a problem. Will there be a job at the end of all that studying? Why not leave school at the earliest possible date and make quick money from some dead-end work? The standard 'I dunno' can exasperate the parent who is asking for the fifteenth successive month, 'What would you like to do when you leave school?'

d. Spiritual pressures

The twin spiritual temptations common to adult Christians are especially acute in the time of youth, namely *licence* and *legalism* — opposite extremes or, more accurately, two sides of the same counterfeit coin. The genuine coin is *life* in the Spirit.

The young person who is so strict about attendance at every meeting even if his parents say they are too tired to go can be self-indulgent in other ways.

> *'________ ____ ______ __________, and you will not gratify the desires of the sinful nature . . . if you are ______ ____ ______ __________, you are not under law.'*
>
> (Galatians 5:16, 18)

The acts of 'the flesh' include:

> *'sexual immorality, impurity and debauchery; idolatry and witchcraft; hatred, discord, jealousy, fits of rage, selfish ambition, dissensions, factions and envy; drunkenness, orgies, and the like'.*
>
> (Galatians 5:19-21)

2. Parental Assistance

a. Pray for them in faith

Job's regular custom (Job 1:4-5) was to present his sons and daughters before the Lord and pray for them after every party in case they had sinned and cursed God in their hearts. However, he later admitted that his practice arose out of anxiety rather than faith. When he lost them all at a celebration in the eldest son's house, he confessed:

> *'What I__________ has come upon me; what I______________ has happened to me.'*
>
> (Job 3:25)

But faith-inspired prayer is something else. We could write a book of the testimonies we know of prodigal sons who have come back to God through the faithful prayers of their parents.

b. Support them 'from the wings'

Remain unthreatened by their changing fancies. By retaining self-control you can teach them to handle their own anger. Don't let them hook your own internal 'child'. Here father and mother can help each other to stay objective. The chances are that your teenager vents his frustration on you, not because he believes you are at fault, but because he feels safe to let rip about a hang-up caused by something outside the home.

Be available to help and advise, but don't be afraid to let them learn some lessons the hard way. And, remember, unsought advice can sound like criticism and condemnation. Make time over a meal or on a drive to open up personal conversations, otherwise they will throw the emergency question at you just as they say goodbye. Stay accessible even when they have left home for college.

Maintain physical contact: he may be too old for mother's kisses but he may still like to have his back massaged.

Teach them respect by showing respect for their opinions and their friends. Even when you disagree, try to understand their reasoning. Supply facilities for bringing their friends home. Train them in trust: tell them where you are going and when you plan to be back if you want them to do the same.

Breed love into them: unconditional love will nurture that emotional child behind the pseudo-adult bravado. How often has Rosemary got out the iron and ironing-board in response to the doomsday crisis: 'Mum, this blouse is creased and I haven't done my hair and I'll be late!' when Hugh was tempted to say, 'That girl will only learn to think ahead if she has to wear it crumpled!' *Ask* their co-operation in duties like babysitting the younger children, gardening, repairs and washing-up.

Set limits — a deadline for coming home, for their own safety. Too much responsibility can overwhelm. They will probably be relieved to have the excuse 'My father will murder me if I'm late home' just as the college or office party starts getting sensual.

Hold them close — but with an open palm. Beware of breeding an unhealthy dependence, e.g. the only child of a widow.

c. Supply them with practical information

Share from your own experience of when you were his age. Testify how others, now up in the pavilion balcony, coped with their pressures and made a good innings (Hebrews 12:1, 'such a great cloud of witnesses', namely, the heroes and heroines of faith of Hebrews 11). The balcony-voices help to drown out the rattling of the skeletons of doubt in the cellar cupboards!

Rather than criticise and accuse, tell him how you *feel* about some of his actions and reactions. 'You may have a fourteen-year-old daughter yourself one day, son,' Hugh cautioned one of our lads about his first sign of 'puppy love'.

Speak faith and hope from God's Word into their fears and despair. Encourage and affirm every good point of theirs, don't just speak when you disagree.

Explain to them what's happening to their moods through hormonal fluctuations.

Without being heavy or legalistic, warn of what spirits operate in the extreme elements of the modern music scene.

d. Impart wisdom into all four dimensions of their development

Father and mother need to confer together on all policies. They need to spend more time together now because of the new complexities that lie ahead.

Update your own prejudices:

☐ Do you want him to get a degree because you never had the opportunity yourself?

☐ Do you tell him off for some of his behaviour just because it embarrasses you?

☐ Are you informed about their interests and activities? Hugh went to Hallé orchestra concerts with our girls because both he and they enjoyed classical music; but he also sat and watched *Top of the Pops* with the boys to discover what was good, bad and indifferent in the type of music he would not instinctively choose — and found much that he did enjoy. It is OK to have preferences but immature to hold prejudices

1. *Physical wisdom (especially about their emotions)*

☐ Explain that we *all* have emotional cycles

☐ Help him to set worthwhile, achievable goals

☐ Suggest how she can diversify her interests

2. *Mental wisdom (especially self-esteem)*

☐ Assure him that God is for him. Talk him out of letting the enemy determine his self-image. The ten despondent spies viewed themselves as the giants of Canaan saw them:

> *'We seemed like grasshoppers in our own eyes, and we looked the same to them.'*
>
> (Numbers 13:33)

☐ Help her to compensate for weaknesses by achieving success in other areas

☐ Encourage them to confide in a reliable adult outside the family who can give them a more objective 'second opinion'

☐ Inculcate self-discipline: to get up in time for work, even adults need a respectable bedtime

☐ Respect her privacy: don't pry into her diaries and correspondence

3. Social wisdom

- ☐ Teach him to say 'No' politely, as did Daniel and his friends (see Daniel 1)

- ☐ Train him in the right use of humour — to laugh *with* people, not *at* them; to make himself the butt of the joke

- ☐ Show her how to budget; economical use of the family phone and car, etc.

- ☐ Let them opt out of some family events. She may be bored with blackberrying; he may find Great-Aunt Gertie's cucumber sandwiches less exciting than watching a video at home

- ☐ Help him choose a career

- ☐ Apprentice them in the art of discerning character when they make new friends

- ☐ Instruct them how to 'date'

- ☐ Teach your son how to ask a girl out, to go to her home to collect her and meet her parents, how to order a meal, etc.

- ☐ Teach your daughter how to refuse an offer of a date politely; how to escape if he tries to take advantage; to bring him home for coffee; and especially how to make him 'work' for her hand in marriage, just as Jacob served seven years for Rachel! He will appreciate your daughter all the more if he has to practise some old-fashioned chivalry and *real* romance

And let them know how parents feel about giving away a daughter: 'It's like giving away my Stradivarius to a gorilla; like mother wren letting her brood lodge with the neighbourhood cat!'

4. Spiritual wisdom

- ☐ The adage 'If you don't stand for something you'll fall for anything' is true. Encourage them to stand alone, like Daniel when thrown to the lions, and his friends when tossed into the fiery furnace (Daniel 6 and 3)

- ☐ Apply the practical wisdom of the book of Proverbs to the practical decisions of life

☐ Discourage grumbling and complaining — they take us away from God's presence (Romans 1:21-24) whereas thanksgiving and praise usher us into his presence (Psalm 100:4) and make our witness effective in society (Philippians 2:14-15)

☐ Give them spiritual goals to fight for. Remember, it is the time of life when they need a challenge and love a cause to champion, like David against Goliath!

> *'You, young men . . . are strong, and the word of God lives in you, and you have overcome the evil one.'*
>
> (1 John 2:14)

****

LESSON 7

Transition Through Teens

True or False

1. T F Adolescence is just the same as every other stage in growing up.
2. T F Boredom and depression are not uncommon among teenagers in general.
3. T F Most teenagers have to re-examine their beliefs.
4. T F Idealism is a characteristic of youth. They love to have a cause to champion.
5. T F Legalism and licence spring from very different spiritual roots.
6. T F When a child reaches his thirteenth birthday his parents should cancel all rules. He must make all his own decisions from now on.
7. T F To impose strict homecoming times after the age of sixteen is unreasonable.

8. T F It is a mistake to base parental rules merely on prejudice.
9. T F Teenagers should not get counsel from anyone outside the home.
10. T F Grumbling and complaining are not just psychological symptoms but spiritual failings.

Group Discussion

1. Exchange observations of pressures common to the teen years.
2. Tell each other of lessons you have learned first hand or from others that have changed your own attitudes and behaviour towards adolescents.
3. Discuss: 'We need to let them out of the cage but keep them on a long lead.'

Personal Assignment

1. Examine your own reactions and assess whether some of your preferences are not in fact prejudices.
2. Make a list of areas you intend to adjust when handling your teenagers.
3. Write a letter to each of your teenagers (or an imaginary letter to your future teenagers) asking them to help you understand how they feel and in what ways you could help them better. Express your pride in them and desire for their greatest blessing.

True or False

1.F 2.T 3.T 4.T 5.F 6.F 7.F 8.T 9.F 10.T